Famine *150*

COMMEMORATIVE LECTURE SERIES

TEAGASC / UCD

Famine *150*

COMMEMORATIVE LECTURE SERIES

Edited by
Cormac Ó Gráda

University College
Dublin

Co-ordinator Famine 150
commemorative lecture series and exhibition,
John Keating, Teagasc

1997

Teagasc.
19 Sandymount Avenue
Ballsbridge,
Dublin 4
Tel: +353 1 668 8188
Fax: +353 1 668 8023

ISBN   1 901138 09 7

First published 1997

Cover "Peasants taken away by death" by Alphonse Legros
and reproduced by kind permission of the National Gallery of Ireland.

Design by DBA Publications.

Printed by Leinster Leader.

CONTENTS

CONTRIBUTORS

Mary E. Daly: Associate Professor and Head, Combined Departments of History, University College Dublin. Author of *The Great Famine in Ireland* (Dublin, 1986), *Industrial Development and Irish National Identity, 1922-1939* (Syracuse and Dublin, 1992) and many other books and articles.

David Dickson: Senior Lecturer and Head of Department of Modern History, Trinity College, Dublin. Author of many articles and co-editor of several books on eighteenth and nineteenth century Irish economic and social history. Author of *New Foundations: Ireland 1660-1800* (Dublin, 1986).

Leslie J. Dowley: Head, Plant Pathology and Entomology Department, Teagasc, Oakpark Research Centre, Carlow. Ireland's leading expert on blight control strategies, an area in which he has published widely.

Andrés Eiríksson: Born in Iceland, he is currently a researcher with the National Famine Research Project based in Trinity College, Dublin. He is also co-author of *Estate Records of the Irish Famine: A Second Guide to Famine Archives.*

Laurence Geary: Currently lecturing in the History Department at University College Cork. Specialises in the social history of medicine in nineteenth century Ireland.

John Joseph Lee: Head of the Department of History, University College Cork, and Senator. Author of T*he Modernisation of Ireland 1848-1918* (Dublin, 1973) and *Modern Ireland 1918-1985* (Cambridge, 1990) and many other works.

Cormac Ó Gráda: Associate Professor, Department of Economics, University College Dublin. Author of Ireland: *A New Economic History* (Oxford, 1994) and *An Drochshaol: Béaloideas agus Amhráin* (Dublin, 1994).

Peter M. Solar: Lectures at Vesalius College, Vrije Universiteit van Brussel. Author of many articles on Irish and European economic history.

INTRODUCTION

The arrival in Ireland of *Phytophthora infestans,* the potato blight, in the summer of 1845 did not mark the true beginning of the Great Famine. Few, if any, died as a result of that first attack, which was partial and occurred late in the growing season. Nor, as they sowed their potatoes in the spring of 1846, did the people who had become so reliant on the potato believe it would recur. Had the blight passed on to some other clime during the winter, the following year's potatoes would have been safe and there would have been no catastrophe. In that event, the 'famine' of 1845 would have been like the minor famines of 1822 or 1831, the stuff of specialist histories. Still, though nobody at the time could have known it, the die was cast as soon as the first leaves and stalks began to blacken in August and September 1845.

There was to be no cure for this new mysterious fungus. This was the logic behind beginning the sesquicentennial commemoration of the Great Famine in 1995. The beginning was spontaneous and truly popular. Even for those academics who argued on historical grounds that opting for 1995 was 'jumping the gun', there could be no holding back. The commemoration spawned a bewildering series of lectures, summer schools, conferences at home and abroad, radio and television programmes, publications, and many other special commemorative events.

The only problem with the choice of 1995 were some signs of a new kind of 'famine fatigue' by year's end. By November one journalist stated that "it's hard not to feel that, really, it's all been said by now", while another claimed in December that "the arguments had been thrashed to death". [1] Among Irish Americans there was talk of being 'famined-out'. The sentiment is understandable. Yet, in truth, much about the Great Famine remains hidden, waiting to be discovered and studied. In 1995 most of the discussion dwelt on the more familiar issues of narrative, relief, politics, and culpability, while other important aspects were largely ignored. It is to be hoped that during the next few years the commemorations and research will focus interest on new issues, some of which were raised but not resolved during 1995. This volume reproduces the series of eight lectures on the Famine delivered to large and lively audiences in the Concourse Hall of the RDS in Ballsbridge, between 14 September and 28 September 1995. The series was jointly organised by Teagasc and University College Dublin, in conjunction with Teagasc's highly successful *Famine 150* Commemorative Exhibition. As befits Teagasc's educational and scientific functions, the series had a bias towards social and agricultural aspects.

This brief introduction is not the place for yet another summary of the catastrophe that was the Irish Famine. The topic is well covered in some of the specialist books published in the course of 1995, in particular those by Christine Kinealy and Peter Gray, and in the collections of Thomas Davis and Radio na Gaeltachta lectures edited by Cathal Póirtéir. Those works re-establish the centrality of the Famine in Irish and European history, they give due scope to its catastrophic dimension, and they draw attention to the unfriendly ideological and awkward economic contexts in which it happened. Instead, I will seek to explain how this collection adds to our knowledge of the Great Famine.

The potato has played a far greater role in Irish history than in the history of any other European country. In Ireland, for several decades in the late eighteenth and early nineteenth centuries it either prompted or accommodated - interpretations differ - the fastest population growth in western Europe. Moreover, while the potato would later be associated with Irish backwardness, in the seventeenth and eighteenth centuries, the Irish were seen as innovators in potato cultivation. John Forster's interesting account suggests that the potato was well known in parts of Ireland before it became popular in England:

These Roots, although they came at first from the Indies, yet thrive and prosper very well in Ireland, where there is whole Fields of them; from whence they have been brought into Wales and into the North Parts of England, where they likewise prosper and increase exceedingly. They are in quality temperate, very agreeable and amical to the Nature of Man, and of a good and strong nourishment.

That was in 1664. The potato was introduced into Scotland from Ireland "towards the end of seventeenth century ... but very sparingly cultivated for more than sixty years". A further gloss on the potato's role in Ireland is given by the Irish emigré Thomas Keating who, in Year II of the French Revolution, deemed it a patriotic duty to advise the French on the advantages of the potato. This is a reminder that as late as the 1790s the potato was little cultivated throughout much of France.

Small wonder that the potato came to be known as the 'Irish potato'. In early nineteenth century English cartoons the Irish and the potato seemed synonymous. Yet in Ireland today few remember the potato for what novelist Maria Edgeworth saw as "the thousands of hardy bodies and merry souls which have blessed the potato". The potato evokes instead one of the greatest human disasters of the nineteenth century.

Why did the Irish place more of their trust in the potato than the Scots, the French, or the Scandinavians? Was it simply because they were poorer, was it because Ireland suited the potato particularly well? Or was it partly a matter of culture too? The Irish seem to have cultivated the potato as a garden crop from the outset, but in parts of Europe the potato seems to have been introduced first as a fodder crop. Did this delay its adoption as food for humans in certain areas? For how long before the Famine had Irish reliance on the root been greater? Several historians including Ken Connell, Louis Cullen, and most recently the late Austin Bourke have dwelt on such issues. In his contribution to this volume, David Dickson provides his own insights into these questions in an original and authoritative account on the potato before the Famine.

Mary Daly's sharp analysis of the state of agriculture on the eve of the Famine complements Dickson's study. She modifies the traditional picture of a subsistence-driven farming sector, pointing to high yields per acre and other signs of 'improvement'. Yet the system that had evolved before 1845 was heavily dependent on cheap labour and on the potato, and with the visitation of *Phytophthora infestans* its days were numbered. Daly interprets Irish agricultural policy in the twentieth century as a doomed attempt "to recreate or shore up the residues of pre-Famine Ireland".

Though there had been harvest failures before 1845, nothing in the potato's past could have prepared the Irish for the ravages of 1845-48. Leslie Dowley provides a scientist's perspective on the potato blight's early impact and on the controversies provoked.

Relatively few died of literal starvation during the Great Famine; dysentery, typhus, typhoid fever, and other hunger-induced infectious diseases did most of the damage. When disease struck, there was little that medical knowledge *per se* could contribute. Isolation in fever hospitals was the main institutional remedy for fever. Medical 'remedies' are likely to have done more harm than good. A contemporary account described treatment of famine-related diseases in Dublin as follows:

> Plenty of nourishment and the free use of stimulants were found to be absolutely necessary. Wine was freely given, and with the best effects. General experience was decidedly opposed to the use of bleeding in any form. In some cases of local congestion the application of a few leeches, or the abstraction of a small quantity of blood by cupping-glasses, was found beneficial. Mercury was only given as a mild aperient or alternative, and sometimes, combined with Dover's powder, in dysentric cases it acted beneficially. Opium does not appear to have been very generally employed; "it was only useful for allaying the vomiting of the secondary fever." "A combination of morphia and tartar emetic was found so valuable in cases of excitement and delirium, that it was styled a specific in the North Union sheds."

In late 1848, from its headquarters in Dublin, the Board of Health recommended a variety of "powders" for cholera victims: they included a compound of chalk and opium - "one powder every half hour until the looseness ceases" - and pills of mercury and opium. Against dysentery and diarrhoea, the eminent medical man, William Stokes, recommended doses from a concoction of whiskey and laudanum diluted in 2 gallons (9 litres) of water, to which 2 lbs. (0.9 kg) of logwood chippings had been added before boiling and cooling down. The relevant aspects of scientific medicine were still far in the future in the 1840s. The importance of cleanliness in the homes and yards of the poor was understood, and the link between contaminated food and water and dysentery stressed. But his clinical experience led a doctor at the Hardwick Street fever hospital to surmise whether "the epidemic, like the ague, owes its origin to terresterial miasms?", and in an attack on other Dublin medical men who held that famine conditions caused fever, the editor of the *Dublin Medical Press* thought "it could easily be shown that famine and destitution are more frequently the effect than the cause of fever".

Modern medical wisdom would not rate such diagnostics or treatments highly; indeed, some of them (such as cupping) were likely to further weaken already weak patients, and some (such as mercury) were positively harmful. But, on the whole, did medical treatment save lives during the Famine?.

The answer to the question is probably no. Effective antidotes were lacking for another half-century or more: doctors simply could not cure infectious diseases. Indeed they died in large numbers themselves (as did the clergy and others who came into regular contact with the destitute in the course of their work). How much difference would better medical knowledge have made? Would the famished simply not have died of something else? These are difficult questions. In his contribution, Laurence Geary provides his own considered answers and indicates where further research might lead.

Cormac Ó Gráda's and Peter Solar's papers add a comparative

and international dimension to the proceedings. Ó Gráda shows that while the horrific symptoms of famine have changed little since the 1840s, the dimensions and the causes have. A comparative perspective highlights the relative size of the Irish Famine in the world history of famines. Peter Solar reminds us that the failure of the potato after 1845 produced hardship and indeed excess mortality in other parts of Europe too. Excess mortality was considerable in Belgium and the Netherlands, for instance. Solar's paper ranges far and wide across those parts of Europe where the potato was important, and allows him to answer why so many died in Ireland from a novel perspective.

Andrés Eiríksson's contribution gives the lie to Michael Davitt's accusation of 'wholesale cowardice' against the poor for not resisting during the Famine. However, the unrest that Eiríksson describes is different than that envisaged by Davitt, being largely local and too uncoordinated to be effective. Eiríksson also offers a novel and persuasive explanation for why such protest died out in the summer of 1847.

In the last lecture in the *"Famine 150"* series, reproduced as the final paper in this collection, Joseph Lee offers a critical overview of Irish famine historiography. Claiming that historians were less negligent than sometimes alleged, he gives due credit to pioneers such as the contributors to the collaborative enterprise directed by Dudley Edwards and Desmond Williams, to the Israeli-American economic historian Joel Mokyr, and to the late Austin Bourke.

Finally, I would like to thank John Keating and Liam Downey of Teagasc for their support throughout, as well as those who chaired and contributed to the discussion at the various sessions at the RDS.

Cormac Ó Gráda
Dublin, December 1996

Note
1. John Boland in the *Sunday Business Post,* 26 November, 1995; Eddie Holt in the *Irish Times,* 30 December, 1995

THE POTATO AND IRISH DIET BEFORE THE GREAT FAMINE

David Dickson

The starting point for much of the recent writing on the pre-Famine world has been to stress the natural abundance of the soil of Ireland, the nutritional adequacy of Irish diets, and the remarkable growth in the total volume of Irish food exports that had occurred since the mid-eighteenth century. Thus it can be argued that, even though the island was supporting unprecedented numbers of both humankind and livestock in the pre-Famine generation, the Malthusian ceiling, the maximum sustainable population, had not been reached in 1845 and that Ireland, larder of Britain's Industrial Revolution, could have supported many millions more than the eight it had.

A casual reading of some of the recent literature would imply that there had been no deterioration in nutrition, no disimprovement in the aggregate standard of living since 1800, thus making the Great Famine seem all the more bizarre and unexpected.[1] Indeed, the estimates by Cormac Ó Gráda and others on adult Irish heights, life expectancy, and trends in agricultural output and productivity can be used to construct an essentially optimistic, upbeat assessment of pre-Famine society.[2]

However, a rejection of older assumptions that early nineteenth century Ireland was a 'runaway' society, a necessarily doomed economy, does not imply that it was a wealthy society or one without great structural problems, for we are dealing with a society in which the degree of inequality was extreme. Per capita incomes at perhaps £10 per annum were probably towards the lower end of the west European league table, but the skewed pattern of income distribution and the polarisation of wealth was even more abnormal by the standards of the Atlantic rim of Europe.

Perhaps as much as two-thirds of the retained income of unskilled wage-earners was spent on food.[3] And while we can see that the long march of the Irish economy towards tighter integration with its booming neighbour across the Irish Sea benefited the commercial farmer and enriched the landlord, it also contributed to the long-term fall in living standards of the rural labourer and the proto-industrial worker. The very high rates of Irish population increase evident from the middle of the eighteenth century until the 1820s served to reinforce this process of social stratification.[4]

It is only in the final phase of the population growth cycle - the 1830s and 1840s - that evidence on agriculture, food supply, diet and the vital rates of national population begin to become abundant. Everyone seeking for explanations of the Great Famine faces a resulting problem: how can we reconstruct the evolution of Irish society from, say, the early 1700s, when all the best sources come from the end of that period, the immediate pre-Famine years? Many years ago the geographer T.W. Freeman wrote a book called *Pre-Famine Ireland* which was simply a snapshot of the country, its landscapes, its social geography in the 1830s and 1840s; he made no real attempt to look back into the eighteenth century and use his evidence to infer previous trends.[5] This is precisely what an American economic historian, Joel Mokyr, did seek to do in his book *Why Ireland Starved* in 1982; his study demonstrated the possibilities of extrapolating from this statistics-rich period. Others have been slow to build on his approach.[6]

Which brings us finally to our main concern: there is probably more evidence on what Irish people were eating on the eve of the Great Famine than at any time in Irish history, at least until the modern introduction of household budget surveys. This is thanks principally to a remarkable social survey, the so-called Poor Inquiry of 1835-36, which among many other things carried out the first large-scale enquiry into food consumption: the parliamentary commission whose brief was to set recommendations for a national system of poor relief, received written answers from over 2,000 respondents (mainly gentry and clergymen) in over a thousand parishes to the question: "what is the ordinary diet ... of the labouring classes of your parish?" The answers varied from the single word 'potatoes' to short essays such as that supplied by Father O'Shea, parish priest of Sts. Peter and Paul in Cork city:

> The labourers generally speaking [live] on potatoes and milk in the morning, and the same in the afternoon and night meals, with the addition or substitution of some dried fish or coarse butcher's meat on two or three days in the week; the tradesmen when at all comfortable use bread and tea, with the additional luxuries of butter and eggs at breakfast; often but not *always* [tradesmen have] flesh meat or fish at dinner; and for supper, something light as tea &c ... I speak only of those who cultivate moral, temperate and prudent habits; there are innumerable and melancholy exceptions (occurring more frequently among the tradesmen than among the common labourers) where their whole history and description may be summed up as a disgusting union of drunkenness, squalidness, both in habitation and dress, and a species of protracted famine - the result, often, of their own want of principle or forethought; often too, of unforeseen and unavoidable calamity.[7]

Such submissions, however intrinsically interesting, are rather hard to fit into a standardised database. However, two social historians in Belfast, Margaret Crawford and Leslie Clarkson, devised a method of content analysis which allowed them classify some 1,569 of the answers supplied to the Poor Inquiry relating to, in all, 65 per cent of the parishes of Ireland, and their results were published some years ago in map and tabular formats.[8]

A POTATO DINNER, CAHIRCIVEEN.

Sitting down to a potato dinner, Cahirciveen, Co. Kerry. February 1846.

The original information, as we have just seen, is descriptive in form and has many limitations. It certainly cannot be used to construct quantitative estimates of calorific intake. Thus, the currently accepted estimates of potato consumption on the eve of the Famine - the 70 potatoes a day consumed by the adult male - are derived from a quite different kind of evidence, namely the national crop returns collected for the 1841 census - on the basis of which the late Austin Bourke calculated how the country's 2.2 million acres of potatoes must have been divided up between man, beast, seed and wastage.[9] These remarkable potato consumption estimates in fact rest on a series of rather speculative assumptions, notably on the key question of potato yields; we should perhaps be rather more cautious as to per capita potato consumption levels until more research is done.

However, what is important for us now is that the Poor Inquiry survey as analysed by Crawford and Clarkson does offer a remarkably nuanced picture of lower-class diets: it confirms the unqualified centrality of the potato in four-fifths of Irish counties, and its importance in the remainder in conjunction with oatmeal; it reveals some marked regional differences in the relative importance of milk, fish and butter and highlights the very narrow range of these dietary supplements, particularly in (a) most southern and western counties, and (b) a number of central and eastern areas where, among other things, domestic (i.e. cottage) industry was in terminal decline. It reinforces the evidence for greater dietary diversity in Ulster and in the inner hinterland of Dublin.

The Crawford-Clarkson analysis provides a lone snapshot of the eating habits of roughly the bottom third of the population - the households of agricultural labourers, low status crafts people, and micro-farmers in the West and on poor soils elsewhere. But does this dietary 'doomsday book' allow us to look backwards, does it in particular help us to understand the remarkable transformation in Irish subsistence which had brought the potato to its monocultural supremacy in the 1830s? Can one detect in the distribution maps Crawford and Clarkson have culled from the Poor Inquiry vestigial survivals of a pre-potato cuisine? Before we seek to answer such questions we need to establish the outlines of earlier Irish diet - but this involves us in a long journey back from the nineteenth century.

Cooking traditions

At the end of the Middle Ages - in sixteenth century Ireland - there were two cooking traditions, one relating to the grass-abundant environment of Ireland where cattle had been the primary criterion of wealth, the other to the probably equally long history of subsistence cereal cultivation - the cow and the plough. The former diet centred on butter, milk (both cow's and sheep, whole and skimmed) and cheeses; the latter on pulses and cereals, in particular oats (a rain-tolerant cereal) which had always been more important than winter-sown wheat or bere barley; it could be boiled in an unground state as gruel, or ground into meal and baked on the open hearth as unleavened bread or 'cake'.[10]

Up to the seventeenth century, environment and culture had determined the balance between these two traditions, with 'white meats' [i.e. dairy products] being more important in the Gaelic and Gaelicised regions - and in upland districts generally, cereals and pulses more prominent in the east, in other words those areas within the influence of the old Anglo-Norman colony. We know all too little of the varieties of porridge and bread, cheeses and curds, and whether they were flavoured with honey or herbs, eaten fresh or fermented. Some sense of the essentially composite character of popular diet in early seventeenth century Munster is suggested by a comment in the famous satirical attack on the lower orders, 'Pairlement Chloinne Tomais', the first part of which was written in the 1610s: the author depicts a churls' feast after battle and suggests a truly Hogarthian scene: everyone received "a fresh, bent-edged, black and badly kneaded barley-cake" and "a heavy thick-bottomed tankard of buttermilk ... and condiment in the shape of chunks of rancid butter, made from the milk of sheep and goats, full of curly hairs, blue pock-marks and tawny beetles...". [11]

The Londoner John Dunton's description of the foods he was given in Connemara in the 1690s is not dissimilar: milk and its by-products in a variety of forms were ever present; thus one meal began with oaten cake being set next to him and:

> at the lower end of our stool or table was placed a great roll of fresh butter of three pound at least, and a wooden vessel full of milk and water. Then enters the landlady's daughter ... she brought the hare

swimming in a wooden bowl full of oil of butter. I told my guide they were very generous in affording so much sauce to the dry meat, but he answer'd me that was but the broth for they boiled it in butter ... in another cabin ... .[12]

Specifically commenting on the diet of one hearth households across the country in the 1670s, Sir William Petty's famous cameo also echoes the earlier satire:

The diet of these people is milk, sweet and sour, thick and thin, which is also their drink in summer-time, in winter small-beer or water ... their food is bread in cakes ... muscles, cockles and oysters, near the sea; eggs and butter very rancid, by keeping in bogs. As for flesh they seldom eat it... .[13]

Petty also noted the winter importance of the potato, but we will return to that. In all, we can adjudge early modern Irish diets to have been poor by European standards in terms of the variety of regularly consumed items, but nutritionally adequate in normal times. Our evidence however is very skimpy, and future research may alter the picture considerably.

Moving forward from the early 1600s we can be fairly certain that the massive shifts in land ownership in seventeenth-century Ireland and the stream of settlers that crossed from Britain did not destroy existing systems of food production or the means of subsistence. Admittedly war in the late sixteenth century, in the 1640s and in 1689-91, had all the appalling 'collateral' consequences of early modern conflicts, but in times of peace the Irish population grew strongly, most noticeably in the early seventeenth century.[14]

Ireland was a net exporter of foodstuffs in most years of the century for which data are extant, with at different stages live cattle, butter, salted beef and cereals being shipped out. The quantities by later standards were small, but the regularity of this trade is nevertheless suggestive. By contrast with its immediate neighbours

Tending the potato ridges at Kinsale circa 1750.

which were more seriously affected by the climatic irregularies associated with the onset of the Little Ice Age, Ireland was successful in avoiding really severe nationwide famines, although major regional food failures did occur during peacetime on at least four occasions, in the 1620s (twice), the 1670s and the 1680s.

Catastrophic cereal harvests over two or more years were the usual ingredient, although a conjunction of cereal losses and fodder shortages was the most deadly cocktail: thus in mid-summer 1674 Archbishop Oliver Plunkett of Armagh reported that "thousands upon thousands" of families in his ecclesiastical province (i.e. Ulster and north Leinster) had left their home to scavenge and beg for food and blamed this on the grain and fodder scarcity of the preceding year, which had been compounded by the destruction of the young winter-sown crops and the death of "all sorts of animals which were the wealth of the poor Irish people" during the spring of 1674. By September he was reporting that more than 500 had died from hunger in his diocese. Interestingly, Plunkett linked the distress of his flock to the fact that in Ulster "all the good land is in the hands of the Protestants, and the poor Catholics occupy the mountains and the uplands ...". [15]

The potato puzzle

Where into this scenario does the coming of the potato fit? Historians have had great difficulty in determining just how and when it became absorbed into the rural Irish diet, and also why was it so precociously successful in Ireland. Redcliffe Salaman in his global study of the potato's history published in 1949, and all before him, rather uncritically opted for an early and swift incorporation of the potato into popular Irish consumption, whereas Ken Connell's much more conservative estimation (in 1950) set the tone for modern writing. Even Austin Bourke's three stage chronology of its adoption - the potato as novel garden supplement (1590-1675), the potato as winter food for the poor (1675-1750), and the potato as a full-year staple for small farmer and labourer (after 1750) - implied a faster rate of dietary change than some historians would accept.[16]

The potato puzzle has arisen, at least in part, because regional variations have been rather downplayed in the discussion of seventeenth and eighteenth century dietary change. The quantum of evidence - literary, legal and estate - on dietary patterns and shifts is of course meagre in the extreme. But the strikingly southern provenance of nearly all early references to the potato can hardly be accidental; not only are most of the references to potatoes that have been identified in the 1641 'loyalist' depositions located in Munster, but most of the published comments on the potato in the later seventeenth century - by Gookin, Petty, Robert Boyle, Stevens - were written from a Munster perspective.[17] Why should this be?

Louis Cullen has suggested that the early diffusion of the potato was as a vegetable supplement cultivated principally by the New English settlers - who of course were thick on the ground in many parts of south Munster in the early seventeenth century.[18] This seems likely, but there is circumstantial evidence that the social descent of the potato may already have begun in that region before the 1640s. Does Munster offer us evidence of a direct link between the aggressive policies of New English settlers [Walter Raleigh, Richard Boyle, *et al.*] and the food security of the indigenous population?

Certainly there seems to have been extensive population displacement off the best soils of Cork and Tipperary in the early 1600s as commercial sheep and store cattle production undermined older systems of mixed agriculture. Yet, given the amount of underutilised land in the early days of the Munster Plantation, existing patterns of farming and modes of subsistence should have been transferred fairly easily onto inferior soils and reclaimed land. In other words, it seems unlikely that south Munster's potato precocity could have arisen directly because of its colonial economy. What is more likely to have been important was the region's slightly milder climate, in particular its almost frost-free coastal districts.

The first varieties of the potato available in the seventeenth century were planted in late winter and dug out from July; therefore the prevalence of spring frost was a major factor limiting wider adoption. The maritime rim of Waterford and Cork was to become famous for its early potatoes; it also emerged as the first area to exploit seaweed as a potato fertiliser. By the early eighteenth century a number of coastal parishes from Dungarvan to Glandore specialised in the commercial production of potatoes which were shipped to the urban markets of Dublin and Cork.[19]

Bonnyclabber

Also contributing to the early prominence of the potato in parts of the south was the growth in a wholesale demand for butter from the Munster ports, particularly evident by the 1680s: the switch from subsistence dairying to commercial butter production left a residue product for domestic consumption - *bainne clabair,* anglicised as 'bonnyclabber' - soured and thickened butter-milk, which came to be a central element in the summer and autumn diets of poorer families in dairying districts. Bonnyclabber lacked the food value of whole milk and butter, one of its key deficiencies being vitamin A; however this is present, albeit in modest amounts, in the potato. In the pastoral districts of the south at least, there seems to have been a steady erosion of traditional dairy-centred diets and in its place a mixed diet in which the most important components for more than half the year were the potato mixed with bonnyclabber.[20]

The potato first emerged in the southern province as the centrepiece of winter diet - from August to March, taking the pressure off the late summer wait for the oats harvest. From March until mid-summer or beyond, even among the poorest households in the area, oatmeal played the leading role. This tandem diet of potatoes and oats was to remain the cornerstone of subsistence

The potato seller - Dublin street vendor, c.1770
"Buy my large new potatoes: Here's green pease, young pease;
Young beans, large Windsor beans".

for more than a hundred years. The opportunity cost of sticking with older patterns of eating was too high for all but the most comfortable of tenant farming families, and the new potato/bonnyclabber/oatmeal combination, while regarded as an inferior diet, was almost certainly more nutritious than those which it replaced.[21]

Elsewhere the older diets were more resistant to change. The picture remains somewhat opaque, but it seems that in the first half of the eighteenth century the majority of Ulster and Leinster households were much more ample grain eaters than those in Munster, and indeed that the range of cereals now being cultivated was broader than in the seventeenth century. Wheat, rye and barley were achieving a new importance, both in consumption and sale. Peas and beans were on the retreat. Those areas that had had a strongly dairy-dominated diet in the seventeenth century gradually lost it in the eighteenth - but through greater grain consumption in the first instance. [22] Finally, in Connacht the pattern is particularly shadowy, but one can speculate that there the butter-centred diet lasted longest, giving ground to the potato as store cattle production undermined subsistence dairying.

From the 1650s to the 1720s Ireland was less obviously touched by the Little Ice Age than was either France or Scotland, despite experiencing several terrible winters. Population indices suggest modest growth up to the mid-1680s, and after the War of the Two Kings stop-start growth for another generation. A majority of Irish counties had seen a doubling of their population in the period. However, the two decades from the mid-1720s to the mid-1740s stand out as a major break in this broadly positive scenario.[23]

The second half of the 1720s was marked by a run of appalling grain harvests and this, coupled with international commercial depression, led to extreme food shortages. It is clear that it was lowland Ulster and the Dublin region that were disproportionately affected, in other words the most developed parts of the economy.[24] The stresses of unbalanced growth gave rise to a pauper and fever-stricken inflow into the towns, and the fledgling Dublin press carried a litany of reports of famine-related epidemics; there was an unprecedented civilian emigration, as many as 15,000 may have departed for the American colonies during the 1720s, most of whom were Protestants from rural Ulster. The regionally specific impact of this famine - the areas of the country where oats and winter corn were all important - hints at the importance elsewhere of the potato as a cushion against the effects of defective grain harvests. Those parts of the southern half of the country which now had a famine insurance policy in their potatoes-and-oats tandem diet were, it seems, insulated against the many wet seasons and cold summers of the period.

The Famine of 1740 - 41

There are shadowy references to defective potato crops in one or two years in the 1720s,[25] but nothing to weaken the reputation or popularity of the reliable root until 1739. The country was in a bruised condition after several years of depressed markets and poor harvests when, on 27 December of that year temperatures across Ireland fell far below freezing point and a sinister frost set in. What ensued, here and across most of north-western Europe was - and remains - the most severe period of extreme cold on record.[26] The polar weather lasted almost without remission for seven weeks, keeping the interiors of most houses below freezing, and it was followed by an extraordinary set of freak seasons, starting with a cold and rainless spring so bleak that by late May it was said that the "grass and corn were all burnt up and the fields looked as red as foxes". [27] A cool dry summer was followed by the coldest autumn in two centuries and then by a snowy winter; there was a drought but little heat in the summer of 1741, and normal rainfall patterns only returned nearly two years after the first great frost.[28]

Such a bizarre sequence of climatic aberrations was hard enough for a poor agricultural society to cope with, but it was the overnight disaster at the end of December 1739 that had toppled the first domino and precipitated the crisis. When the great cold struck, nearly all domestic stocks of potatoes were still in the ground or stored in shallow pits. The tubers were universally frosted and thereby rendered inedible. There followed the first great potato-centred crisis in Irish history, and one made all the worse by widespread hypothermia, a huge mortality of cattle, sheep and horses, and a sharp economic recession. Much of the seed corn was diverted into human consumption in the early months of the potato scarcity; thus the cereal

The obelisk at Killiney, Co. Dublin,
erected in 1741 as a private famine employment scheme.

and potato acreages sown and harvested in 1740 were greatly down on those of normal years. And because it was a continent-wide crisis, the usual sources of emergency grain to top up Irish supplies - southern and eastern England, and the southern Baltic - were not sufficient to make up the deficit on this occasion. [29]

The population of the country on the eve of this crisis was in the region of 2.4 million. After the first round of deaths from cold and starvation, tens of thousands were reduced to begging, to wandering along the highways and to collecting the classic foods of famine: docks, cresses, nettles, seaweed and the blood drawn from live cattle. The combination of indigestible and unsustaining food and of dangerously unhygienic living conditions gave rise in the later months of 1740 to a series of overlapping epidemics - typhus, relapsing fever, and dysentery - with mortality peaking in 1741, the year of the slaughter in folk tradition. The Dublin papers in the early months of 1741 commented repeatedly on the march of the killer epidemics across at least three of the four provinces.[30] The scale of this premier mortality crisis can be estimated with greater confidence than for any of the seventeenth century food failures. It was almost certainly worse than any peacetime crisis, perhaps only equalled by the plague and famine of 1647-51 (in the later stages of the Confederate wars and accompanying the Cromwellian re-conquest).[31]

The worst of the suffering in 1740-41 was in the south and west, and Ulster seems to have escaped the great mortality. At least a fifth of the population of Munster and probably between 12.5 and 16 per cent of the population of Ireland overall died from famine-related causes, in absolute terms three to four hundred thousand victims and in relative terms a disaster at least as severe as the Great Famine itself. And whereas the worst mortality in the 1840s was in regions of poor soils and congested population, that in 1740-41 seems to have been in some of the most fertile areas of Munster (east Cork, Tipperary and east Limerick) where an enlarged class of marginalised farmers had in recent decades been squeezed by sheepmasters and land-engrossing cattlemen.[32]

The lessons of 1741, or at least some lessons, were learnt in terms of public policy and private charitable agency.[33] Relatively severe food shortages continued to feature in the second half of the eighteenth century but, and this is the critical point, the years of very high grain prices in that stage seem to have caused only modest rises in local death rates.[34] Other factors strengthening society's capacity to ride out the years of harvest failure were the growth of proto-industrial employment, particularly for women, which gave cash flow and savings where none had been before; infrastructural improvements, which greatly aided the inter-regional movement of grain and the convergence of food markets; and the fact that all households with some control over farmland were benefiting from the long-term rise in agricultural prices which, with interruptions, lasted from the late 1740s until Waterloo 70 years later.

That said, we know surprisingly little about fluctuations in the potato crop at that time, for compared to comments on the grain harvest its performance received scarcely any public notice. Very poor potato crops were publicly noticed in 1765, 1770, 1783 and 1800, but in 1770 alone were there reports of a potato failure not associated with bad grain harvests; no evidence has so far come to light of any regional distress as a result. [35]

Taking this period as a whole - the era Connell christened as "the gap in the famines" - we cannot tell whether the variability of Irish potato output was in fact lower than that of the staple grain crops. It may well be that greater fluctuations in potato yields were occurring than appearances suggest and that these were being masked by excess potato production in normal years - when potatoes surplus to human needs were being fed to the ever growing pig population.[36] Certainly the massive rise in pork and bacon exports from low mid-eighteenth century levels is one indication of the intensification of potato production in the decades before 1800. [37]

The surrender of oatmeal

We also lack direct quantitative measures of the process of widening potato cultivation, but it can be inferred from the interplay of several new elements in the agrarian scene. First, the long-term rise in international cereal prices and the growth of demand from Irish town-dwellers led to a steady, and in some districts spectacular extension of tillage farming, and the standard crop at the beginning of a corn rotation in the eighteenth century was the potato - not as in England the turnip; not only was the potato an admirable cleansing crop in Irish conditions, but it was also by far the best means of reclaiming and breaking in marginal ground. Secondly, the development of new varieties of potato suited to local soils and habitat assisted the growth in potato acreage; the most important breakthrough - in the third quarter of the eighteenth century - was the popularisation of the apple potato which under normal conditions remained edible throughout the year - although only just. [38]

These were essentially positive factors at work, extending the dominance of the potato far outside its original Munster heartland. More ominously - and visible first in Munster - was the eclipse of the spring/summer consumption of oats by labouring and petty landholding families, and the consumption of the potato for all or nearly all the year, supplemented by salted herring in winter, cabbage in summer. For some, the surrender of oatmeal may have been a logical response to the high prices that cereals were commanding in the market; they were adopting another "inferior" diet to maximise cash income as their grand or great-grandparents had abandoned large-scale butter consumption. But for many labourers the increased dependence on the potato was simply a reflection of their falling real wages, or, more concretely, their weakening bargaining power in the annual negotiations with farmers in the labour-for-potato-ground trade-off.

The narrowing of diet had of course the effect of removing the safety net of a second subsistence crop, although many potato-eating small-farm households depended on cereal production for cash income and had therein an emergency reserve food source in the event of a potato deficit. [39]

Not only was oatmeal consumption in retreat before 1800, but skimmed milk and bonnyclabber as well. This was tied up with the changing pattern of cow ownership. A rural family without a cow in earlier times was truly to be pitied - thus references to the poor and their starving cows in years of scarcity. But with the contracting size of labourers' plots in the late eighteenth century, cow ownership was becoming more exclusive to the *bona fide* farming class. Labourers, particularly in villages and towns, resorted to the market for milk, but even that option was being closed for many as milk prices began to rise. [40]

By the time of the Poor Inquiry survey in the 1830s, it was only among the poor of upland parts of Connacht and Ulster that the archaic role of butter could still be found, whereas in Munster, long the epicentre of commercial dairying, not just butter but even milk consumption was a thing of the past for those below the farming class. And only the poor of lowland Ulster retained a tradition of large-scale oatmeal consumption. [41]

As we return to the early nineteenth century, it is imperative to keep in mind not just the regional patterns of dietary evolution, but the class ones as well. It is true that visitors to Ireland were sometimes amazed at the culinary simplicity of the *coqs de village,* the strong farmers, but the general trend in the half century before the Great Famine was for farming families - those controlling anything above say eight acres of ground - to widen their diets; a greater range of vegetables, greater consumption of wheaten bread, perhaps more meat, but still including the ever popular potato, although preferably the drier, more flavoursome varieties. Consumption of tea and sugar by farm families - once the preserve of the towns and gentry - was also becoming visible in the east and north of the country.

The rise of the village grocer's shop, often of course attached to premises licensed for the sale of liquor, which we often think of as one of the novel features of the post-Famine landscape, was already occurring in parts of Ulster and Leinster a generation earlier; for instance it was noted of the parish of Glynn, Co. Antrim in the 1830s that:

> much less meal than formerly is now used, more raw corn now being sent to the market, and the facility of obtaining bakers' bread from the numerous bread carts which traverse the country and supply the petty grocers is so great that bakers' bread being cheaper is gradually superseding the oaten cake. [42]

However, whatever about the rise of bakers' bread, griddle bread and oatcakes survived into the era of photography. But one suspects that much of what is today regarded as traditional Irish cuisine - soda bread, barm brack, boxty, champ, colcannon etc. - was only then being developed in the kitchens of the solid farming class.

Farmers' incomes took a battering after the Napoleonic wars as the long-term rise in cereal prices was reversed, but their overall standard of living was almost certainly rising. The conjunctural poverty evident in the first half of the previous century, when harvest crises had reduced tenant farmers and labourers alike to intense but temporary distress, even to wandering, was becoming a distant memory; in its place the structural poverty and the endemic underemployment of the near landless (and cowless) was now everywhere visible; older patterns of occasional hunger migration were now being replaced by the constant movement of marginal groups.

The diets of all below the farming class, an increasing fraction as the great Irish population spurt increased the pre-existing inequalities in rural society, had therefore become unprecedently narrow at the moment captured in the Poor Inquiry snapshot of the mid-thirties: the potato was now the round-the-year staple for three-eighths of the population in at least 26 counties, supplying them with possibly 90 per cent of their calories.

Nearly two and a half centuries of genetic evolution of potato varieties lay behind this remarkable ascendancy. In that it had improved long-term food security, the potato had contributed to the demographic transformation of Ireland from an underpopulated island with less than a million inhabitants in the 1590s to 8.2 million in the 1840s. In its other roles - as engine of land reclamation and as an agent for the regeneration of arable ground - it had aided agricultural productivity; its nutritional superiority over the old pastoral diets, more emphatically over the pulse/oats diets of the east, had had long-term if undetectable consequences for public health. In all, the potato's very successes had helped to create the conditions which now made Irish society so vulnerable in the event of an unforeseen natural disaster: population growth had contributed to the intense stratification of rural society, while the adaptability of the potato had allowed the landless to keep a toehold on the land - unlike their confreres in neighbouring countries.

The potato's multifunctional role on the eve of the Famine is now well understood, as Mary Daly demonstrates in her paper. And because of the complex interlocking functions of the potato in the Irish agrarian system, a drastic collapse in yields such as was to occur in 1846 was bound to have ramifications far beyond the food supply of the labouring classes. In other words, so central was the potato in the finely tuned world of pre-Famine farming that even if its dietary role had been less pivotal than it was, the impact of the blight-induced collapse in yields would still have been traumatic for the farming classes and those whom they employed. [43]

Despite the arguments of Sir William Wilde and many after him, Ó Gráda had argued persuasively that the potato was not becoming more unreliable in the pre-Famine years. Yield variability may in fact have been declining, and the overall trend in yields per acre rising.[44] Insofar as there was 'famine in the land' in the first 45 years of the nineteenth century it was in spite of rather than because of the potato. In the worse such case, the appalling years immediately after 1815, Irish difficulties were part of a Europe-wide phenomenon. Three preconditions for a mortality crisis were then present: multiple grain harvest failures at home, depleted potato yields, and an external food scarcity delaying importation. But severe as the post-Waterloo crisis was, the excess death rate was modest by the standards of a century previously. The intervention by government on an unprecedented scale in 1816-17, helping countless local voluntary committees, helped to control the public health crisis in most counties.[45]

In the following 30 years there were at least half a dozen runs of bad harvests which stirred government and philanthropic agencies into action, but there seems to have been no large-scale clustering of hunger-induced deaths. Food supply crises between 1818 and 1845 were almost entirely confined to the

Contrasting house interiors reflecting the difference between the poor and the well off farming classes.

western counties, and their duration relatively short. The intensity of 'distress' in such areas was very real, but it was mainly seasonal usually spanning the summer months following a poor potato or oats crop. This was the price being paid by the majority of smallholders in many western communities who had developed an exclusive dependence on the potato and who thus lacked the range of dietary choices that had existed a generation or two earlier; such families now owned little or no cattle (which in former hard times could have been bled or sold off for food purchases); and they held little or no cash reserves as ancillary sources of income (spinning and handloom weaving, kelping and fishing) were withering away.[46]

However, the under-employment of rural labour was a problem common to most counties. Mokyr has estimated the average number of days that a pre-Famine labourer was employed (including both hired and domestic tasks) was about 140 per annum.[47] Under-employment combined with greater dependence on local food markets in summertime created the recurrent pattern of seasonal hunger among the poor that was a distinctively new phenomenon in the early nineteenth century; contemporary literary evidence on the seasonal stress experienced by the poor - hungry July - is so powerful that the possibility of some physiological consequences seems likely.

Yet perhaps the evidence may be biased towards the towns, giving an overly bleak picture; for it was in urban communities like Kilkenny, Bandon, Limerick, Drogheda and in Dublin's Liberties that living standards of the semi-skilled and unskilled declined most palpably after the French wars and where the power of the money-lender and the petty speculator in meal compounded the miseries of a swelling proletariat.

Pre-Famine dietary problems should, however, be kept apart from the analysis of the great crisis itself. The fact that Co. Donegal was one of the areas most frequently the object of official concern as a zone of famine between 1817 and 1839 illustrates this particularly aptly: the county was significantly impoverished by the decline of its linen industry, and was one of the largest sources for pre-Famine transatlantic migrants. Yet the impact of the Great Famine turned out to be far less devastating there than in any other western seaboard county.

This has never been satisfactorily explained, but one factor was the relatively late arrival of the potato in the diet of the poor and the continuing familiarity with oatmeal, even in poorer parts of the county; in other words, the tandem diet of the eighteenth century - which had so often kept famine at bay across the country - survived in the backpocket of Ulster in the 1840s.[48] If we overlook such nuances of regional variety in the pre-history of the Famine, we will continue to be unduly puzzled by the event itself. ▦

References

1. These issues are discussed at greater length in a longer version of this paper (entitled *'Diet, Subsistence Crises and Hunger before the Great Irish Famine'*) delivered to The International Conference on Hunger, New York University, May 1995.

2. Joel Mokyr, Why Ireland Starved: A quantitative and analytical history of the Irish economy 1800-1850, 2nd ed. (London, 1985), esp. chaps. 2, 3 and 10; Mary Daly, *The Famine in Ireland* (Dublin, 1986), pp. 19-33; Cormac Ó Gráda, *Ireland before and after the Famine: Explorations in economic history, 1800-1925,* 2nd ed. (Manchester, 1993), pp. 17-9, 37; Ó Gráda, *Ireland: A new economic history 1780-1939* (Oxford, 1994), esp. chaps, 4 and 5. Cf. L.M. Cullen, 'Malthus, Ireland and famine' (unpublished paper, c.1987).

3. Mokyr, *Why Ireland Starved,* p.27; Ó Gráda, *Ireland before and after the Famine,* pp. 15-6, 26-7, 38; Ó Gráda, *New economic history,* pp. 96-7.

4. For an excellent recent overview of Irish demographic trends in this period see Liam Kennedy & L.A. Clarkson, 'Birth, death and exile: Irish population history, 1700-1921', in B.J. Graham & L.J. Proudfoot, eds. *An historical geography of Ireland* (London, 1993).

5. *Pre-Famine Ireland: A study in human geography* (Manchester, 1956).

6. Mokyr, *Why Ireland Starved,* passim; ibid., 'Irish history with the potato', *Irish Econ. Soc. Hist.. VIII* (1981), 8-29.

7. *Third report of the Commissioners for inquiring into the condition of the poorer classes in Ireland* (Parliamentary Papers, 1836, XXX-I, appendices C and D). The quotations are from Append. C (part 1, supplement, pp.31, 37).

8. L.A. Clarkson & E.M. Crawford, 'Dietary directions: A topographical survey of Irish diet, 1836', in Rosalind Mitchison & Peter Roebuck, eds. *Economy and society in Scotland and Ireland 1500-1939* (Edinburgh, 1988),pp. 171-92.

9. P.M.A. Bourke, 'The use of the potato in pre-Famine Ireland', *Jnl. Stat. Soc. Inquiry Soc. Irl., XII, 6* (1968), 72-96.

10. J. O. Bartley, *Teague, shenkin, and sawney: Being an historical study of the earliest Irish, Welsh and Scottish characters in English plays* (Cork, 1954), pp. 32-3; Caoimhín Ó Danachair, 'Bread', *Ulster Folklife, IV* (1958), 29-32; A.T. Lucas, 'Irish food before the potato', in *Gwerin, III* (1960), 8-43; D.B. Quinn, *The Elizabethans and the Irish* (Ithaca, N.Y., 1966), pp. 62-7; L.M. Cullen, 'Irish history without the potato', *Past and Present,, XL* (1968), repr. in C.H.E. Philpin, ed. *Nationalist and popular protest in Ireland* (Cambridge, 1987), pp. 126-38; ibid., T*he emergence of modern Ireland 1600-1900* (London, 1981), chap. 7; ibid., 'Population growth and diet, 1600-1850', in J.M. Goldstrom & L.A. Clarkson, eds. *Irish population, economy and society: Essays in honour of the late K.H. Connell* (Oxford, 1981), pp. 95-103; ibid., 'Comparative aspects of Irish diet 1550-1850', in H.J.Teuteberg, ed. *European food history: A research review* (Leicester, 1992), pp. 45-55; David Dickson, 'Butter comes to market: The origins of commercial dairying in County Cork', in Patrick O'Flanagan & Cornelius G.Buttimer, eds. *Cork: History and Society* (Cork, 1993), pp. 368-9.

11. N.J.A. Williams, ed. Parlement Chloinne Tomais (Dublin, 1981), p. 78. Cf. Cullen, *Emergence,* pp. 142-5. For other contemporary quotations in similar vein see Ó Danachair, 'Bread', 29; Lucas, 'Irish food', 20-1.

12. 'John Dunton's letters', in Edward MacLysaght, *Irish life in the seventeenth century,* 3rd ed. (Dublin, 1969), p. 332.

13. Sir William Petty, *Tracts chiefly relating to Ireland* (Dublin, 1769), p. 355. Cf. Anon., *The present state of Ireland...* (London, 1673), pp. 151-2. The latter tract is noteworthy for seeking to distinguish between the diets of 'the common sort of people', 'the middle sort of the Irish gentry', and 'the best sort of Irish'. It claimed that the common sort 'do feed generally upon milk, butter, curds and whey, new bread made of oatmeal, beans, barley and peas, and sometimes wheat upon festivals, their bread being baked every day against the fire. Most of their drink is butter-milk and whey; they feed much also upon parsnips, potatoes, and watercress...', those higher up the social scale were said to consume better bread and more alcohol [p. 151].

14. Lucas, 'Irish food', 11-2; Raymond Gillespie, *The transformation of the Irish ecnomy 1550-1700* (Dundalk, 1991), pp. 12-19; ibid., 'The Irish economy at war', in Jane Ohlmeyer, ed. *Ireland from independence to occupation 1641-1660* (Cambridge, 1995), p. 176; Dickson, 'The other great Irish famine', in Cathal Póirtéir, ed. *The great Irish Famine* (Cork, 1995), pp. 51-2.

15. John Hanly, ed. *The letters of St. Oliver Plunkett 1625-1681...* (Dublin, 1979), pp. 404, 407 410, 414. Note that the Third Anglo-Dutch War was an additional factor depressing the Irish economy at this stage. For the link between this crisis and emigration to the West Indies see *A journal of the life, travels, sufferings, and labour of love ... of ... William Edmundson* (London, 1829), pp.70-1.

16. R.N. Salaman, *The history and social influence of the potato* (Cambridge, 1949), chaps. 11 and 12; *K.H. Connell, The population of Ireland, 1750-1845* (Oxford, 1950); Cullen, 'Irish history without the potato', pp. 126-38; Joel Mokyr, 'Irish history with the potato', 8-29; P.M.A. Bourke, *'The visitation of God'?: The potato and the great Irish Famine* (Dublin, 1993), chap.1.

17. Salaman, *Potato,* pp. 224-30; Dickson, 'An economic history of the Cork region in the eighteenth century', (unpublished Ph.D. dissertation, University of Dublin, 1977), pp. 369-71; ibid., 'Ireland and the potato: The first 200 years', (unpublished paper, 1995).

18. Cullen, *Emergence,* p. 159

19. Bourke, *'Visitation of God',* pp. 15-6; Dickson, 'Cork region', pp. 328, 340-1; 377.

20. Connell, *Population,* pp. 154-6; Bartley, *Teague,* pp. 112, 121; Lucas, 'Irish foods', 21-4; Cullen, *Emergence,* p. 149; Clarkson & Crawford, 'Dietary directions', pp. 172, 190; Crawford, 'Subsistence crises and famines in Ireland', in Crawford, ed. *Famine: The Irish experience* (Edinburgh, 1989), pp. 210-1; Dickson, 'Butter', pp. 368-9.

21. Dickson, 'Cork region', pp. 374-6; Mokyr, 'Irish history with the potato', 10; Cullen, *Emergence*, pp. 149, 157-8, 165-6, 170; ibid., 'Malthus, Ireland and famine' (unpublished paper, c.1987); ibid., 'Comparative aspects of Irish diet, 1550-1850', pp. 47-8.

22. Cullen, *Emergence*, pp. 144-5, 150-1, 164-70. In pastoral districts of Ulster such as the Sperrin uplands the switch, at least in summer diet, may have been closer to the Munster pattern - from 'butter, curds, cream, in short, a milk diet in all its various preparations' plus some oatmeal, to a potato-centred diet. John MacCloskey, writing in 1821, saw the major change beginning in the 1760s with the decline of summer transhumance: David O'Kane, ed. *Statistical reports of six Derry parishes*, 1821, by Iohn MacCloskey (1788-1876) (Ballinasreen [Historical Society], 1983), p. 16. For a comment on the strongly dairy character of summer diet in the Rosses district of Co. Donegal in 1753, see J.C.Walker, *An historical essay on the dress of the ancient and modern Irish* (Dublin, 1818), append. p. 199.

23. Cullen, *Emergence*, pp. 169-71; David Dickson, Cormac Ó Gráda & Stuart Daultrey, 'Hearth tax, household size and Irish population change 1672-1821', in *Proc. Royal Irish Academy, LXXXII, C* (1982), 164-9.

24. James Kelly, 'Harvests and hardship: Famine and scarcity in Ireland in the late 1720s', in *Studia Hibernia*, XXVI (1991-2), 65-105.

25. Dickson, 'Cork region', p. 372.

26. Michael Drake 'The Irish demographic crisis of 1740-1' in T.W. Moody, ed., *Historical Studies*, VI (Dublin, 1968), pp. 101-24; John D. Post, *Food shortage, climatic variability and epidemic disease in pre-industrial Europe:* The mortality peak in the early 1740s (Ithaca and London, 1985); Dickson, 'Other great famine', pp. 50-9, 259-60. For new dendrochronological evidence, see *The Sunday Tribune* (Dublin), 19 March 1995

27. London Advertiser, 24 May 1740, quoted in Post, *Food shortage*, p.68.

28. Post, *Food shortage*, pp. 63-4, 68-9.

29. In addition to the works cited in fn.26, see Cullen, Economic development, 1691-1750, in T.W. Moody and W.E.Vaughan, eds. *A new history of Ireland; IV: Eighteenth-century Ireland 1691-1800* (Oxford, 1986), pp. 145-8; Dickson, Cork region, pp. 622-3.

30. Drake, 'Demographic crisis', pp. 116-7, 121

31. Gillespie, *Transformation*, pp. 12-9; Dickson, 'Other great famine', pp. 51-2

32. Drake, 'Demographic crisis', pp. 121-2; Dickson, 'Cork region', pp. 630-4; Dickson, et al, pp. 165-8; Post, *Food shortage*, pp. 37-8, 96-7, 174-8, 264-6.

33. Samuel Burdy, *The life of the late Rev. Philip Skelton* ... (Dublin, 1792), pp. 196-7; Dickson, 'In search of the old Irish poor law', in Mitchison & Roebuck, *Economy and society*, pp. 153-6; Kelly, 'Harvests and hardship', pp. 65-105; ibid., 'Scarcity and poor relief in eighteenth-century Ireland: The subsistence crisis of 1782-3', in *Irish Hist. Studies*, XXVII, 109 (1992), 38-9, 61-2.

34. Dickson, 'The gap in famines: A useful myth?', in Crawford, ed. *Famine*, pp. 101-6.

35. Cullen has suggested an exclusively potato failure in 1774/75 as well ('Economic Development, 1691-1750', p. 149).

36. Connell, *Population,* pp. 144-5; Cullen, op. cit. pp. 148-50; Dickson, 'Gap in Famines', pp. 105-7

37. Cullen, *Anglo-Irish trade* 1660-1800 (Manchester, 1968), p. 70; ibid., *Emergence,* pp. 151-3; Dickson, 'Cork region', pp. 454-5.

38. Salaman, *Potato,* pp. 253-62; Mokyr, 'Irish history with the potato', 11-3, 28; Cullen, *Emergence,* p. 157; ibid., 'Comparative aspects of diet', p. 46-7; Bourke, *'The visitation of God'*, pp. 16-20, 33-4; Ó Gráda, *Ireland before and after the Famine,* pp. 9-14.

39. *First report of the General Board of Health in the city of Dublin...*(Dublin, 1822), pp. 41-9; Dickson, 'Cork region', pp. 374-7, 400-11; Mokyr, 'Irish history with the potato', 9; Dickson, 'Gap in famines', pp. 104-7; Ó Gráda, *Ireland,* pp. 14-15. For the comparative lateness of references to the lower class cultivation of the cabbage (1690), see Lucas, 'Irish foods', 31.

40. *First rep., Bd. Of Health,* pp. 41-9, append. pp. 3, 9, 16, 23, 30, 35, 54; Cullen, *Emergence,* pp. 156-7, 169-71, ibid., Comparative aspects of diet pp. 48-48, Daly, *Famine,* p. 32.

41. Crawford and Clarkson, 'Dietary directions', pp. 174-82. Cf. Cullen, *Emergence,* pp. 164-7. For the potato and buttermilk regime among the poor in the upland parishes of south Derry in the 1820s, see O'Kane, *Statistical reports by John MacCloskey,* pp. 18-9.

42. This quotation from the Antrim Ordnance Survey memoir for Glynn is taken from Patricia Lysaght, 'When I makes tea, I makes tea': 'Innovation in food - the case of tea in Ireland', *Ulster Folklife,* XXXIII (1987), 45. Lysaght's comments on bread and tea consumption are particularly important (ibid., 44-71). Also Mokyr, 'Irish history with the potato', 11; Cullen, 'Comparative aspects of diet', p. 49; Ó Gráda, *Ireland,* p. 83, 85; W.H. Crawford, 'Provincial town life in the early nineteenth century: An artist's impressions', in Raymond Gillespie and Brian Kennedy, eds., *Ireland: Art into history* (Dublin, 1994), pp. 48-50.

43. Mokyr, 'Irish history with the potato', 29; Crawford and Clarkson, 'Dietary directions', pp. 177-8. Cf. Peter Solar, 'The Great Famine was no ordinary subsistence crisis', in Crawford, *Famine,* pp. 125-9.

44. Ó Gráda, 'Notes on the potato in Ireland and in Europe before and during the Famine' (unpublished paper, 1995). I am grateful to Cormac Ó Gráda for letting me see a copy of this paper.

45. Timothy P. O'Neill, 'The state, poverty and distress in Ireland, 1815-45', (unpublished Ph.D. dissertation, N.U.I. [U.C.D.], 1971), pp. 5-8, 49-61, 82-8, 156-192, 223-4, 250-1, 288-9, 311; Post, *The last great subsistence crisis in the western world* (Baltimore, 1977); Daly, *Famine,* pp. 38-41; Dickson, 'Old Irish poor law', p. 156.

46. Daly, *Famine*, pp. 39-43. For a late reference to the possibility of drawing blood from cattle as a famine food (in 1817), see O'Kane, *Statistical reports by John MacCloskey*, p. 19.
47. Mokyr, *Why Ireland Starved*, p. 215. For a less pessimistic estimate see Daly, *Famine*, pp. 32-3
48. Daly, *Famine*, pp. 31-43; Crawford and Clarkson, 'Dietary directions', pp. 172-3, 181; Bourke, *'Visitation of God'*, p. 21; Ó Gráda, *Ireland before and after the Famine*, p. 26; Christine Kinealy, *This great calamity: The Irish Famine 1845-52* (Dublin, 1994), p. 171; Dickson, 'Derry's backyard: The barony of Inishowen 1600-1850', in Mairéad Donleavy, ed. *Donegal; History and society.*

There were many tumble-down cottages, often shared with livestock, in pre-Famine Ireland.

FARMING AND THE FAMINE

Mary E. Daly

The most common images of pre-Famine agriculture, both then, and indeed now, are of poverty and backwardness. Jonathan Pim's description is typical:

> A county naturally fertile is left almost unimproved and only half cultivated; the fields are undrained; the rivers, left without care, overflow their banks and turn good land into marsh; straggling hedges and uncultivated spots deform the face of the country; the hay or corn, insufficiently secured, is exposed to the weather; and much land capable of culture is left to its natural wildness, or is so ill tilled that it is but little better than waste.[1]

To make the picture bleaker, we are frequently informed that farmers in many areas grew nothing except successive crops of potatoes - a crop which was widely regarded as much inferior to the turnip which was so beloved of English agricultural improvers. Added to this the equipment and farming methods are generally described as primitive: if the Irish no longer tied the plough to the horse's tail, as in the seventeenth century, they are often condemned for using old wooden ploughs instead of iron ploughs, and for doing jobs by hand which were done using machinery elsewhere in the British Isles.

To round off the grim picture, many accounts of pre-Famine Ireland emphasised that there were countless able-bodied young men who were idle for most of the year. Gustave de Beaumont, a French traveller, believed that the majority of the labouring population were "indolent and idle".[2] Alexis de Tocqueville, travelling in the Tuam area in 1835 described seeing:

> five or six men full of health and strength nonchalantly lying on the banks of the brook ... idleness in the midst of so great poverty.[3]

Sir Charles Trevelyan, the senior British civil servant, who never, to the best of my knowledge visited Ireland, apparently believed that many Irish labourers were idle for up to 47 weeks every year:

> a fortnight planting, a week or ten days digging, fourteen days turf cutting suffice for his subsistence. During the rest of the year he is at leisure to follow his own inclinations. [4]

If all the above constitutes a true account of pre-Famine agriculture, it stands to reason that the Famine was a virtually inevitable consequence of the undeveloped state of Irish agriculture, a disaster waiting to happen.

Lazy beds in Achill

How accurate is this picture? The most important point to note about all these descriptions is their cultural starting point. Ireland was not England, or lowland Scotland. Irish land-tenure systems, the Irish diet and Irish agricultural practices all differed from those in England and they were condemned for that reason, often without any deeper examination of the question. The unfortunately-named "lazy beds", which were used to grow potatoes, made perfect sense in a country which was heavily dependent on the spade and lacked the capital to install drainage pipes in most fields.[5] As one early nineteenth century commentator noted, "rude and artificial as it was, (it) protected the potato from excess moisture". Far from being a "lazy" form of cultivation, it required considerable effort with a spade; one source described it as a "laborious system of culture".[6]

The allegedly primitive state of Irish agriculture was, and indeed is, generally blamed on the land-tenure system. The blackest pictures tended to be painted by those who wanted a change in the existing structure of the rural economy, either by introducing some form of tenant right, or by replacing the lackadaisical landlords, sub-divided holdings and the cottier population with more commercially-aware landlords, larger farmers and wage-earning landless labourers. But pointing out that the analysis is politically-determined does not necessarily mean that it is incorrect. Let us look at the facts.

Some parts of the picture are undoubtedly correct. Tidiness, straight hedges, neat cottages were few and far between in pre-Famine Ireland. The aesthetic appearance of the Irish countryside left much to be desired. There were many tumble-down cottages, often shared with livestock, and the manure heap generally stood at the front door and ocasionally inside in the cabin. The poverty of much of the rural peasantry is equally undeniable. Yet poverty and untidiness are not necessarily syonymous with economic backwardness - Manhattan Island in the late twentieth century springs readily to mind. It is best to judge Irish agriculture by more objective standards.

Agricultural output

Perhaps the most important starting point is agricultural output. Ireland, on the eve of the Famine was capable of feeding 9.5 to 10 million people, 8-8.5 million in Ireland, the remainder via exports to England.[7] The best available estimates of Irish agricultural output on the eve of the Famine suggest that almost two-thirds was contributed by tillage products.[8] Comparing agricultural output in Scotland and Ireland in the mid-1850s, the earliest date when such a comparison can be made, Peter Solar concluded that "crop yields in Ireland generally exceeded those in Scotland". He also believed that Irish crop yields "were likely to have been even higher before the Famine". So much for the supposed superiority of Scottish farming! Moreover Irish yields, like those in Scotland, were high by European standards.[9]

The population had increased steadily over the preceding 100 years; by the 1840s it was probably four times the level of the 1740s. Yet despite occasional threats of food shortage during these years, there is no evidence that significant numbers of people died from lack of food, or from diseases which were spread because of lack of food. Moreover, Irish agricultural exports rose sharply during this period. Trends in agricultural exports and in agricultural output for the 30 years or so immediately prior to the Famine are of particular interest in reaching any assessment of the state of Irish agriculture and on whether the Famine should be seen as a Malthusian crisis.

The Irish population continued to rise until the mid 1840s, though at a slower rate than in the late eighteenth century, and grain exports to Britain rose sharply from an average of 126,000 tons in the years 1813-17 to 450,000 tons by the late 1830s.[10] By 1835 live cattle exports were probably double the level of the early 1820s and they were to double yet again by the eve of the Famine. Sheep exports rose four-fold between the 1820s and the mid 1830s; they too again doubled by 1845. Live pig exports also rose sharply in the decades immediately prior to the Famine.[11] Some of the growth in livestock exports reflects a switch of exports from provisions, i.e. salt beef or salt pork, to livestock.

The livestock trade expanded as a result of improvements in cross-channel shipping; whether this development was of long-term benefit to Irish agriculture is a much-argued point. Nevertheless the picture presented by export data is one of a dynamic, not a stagnant agricultural sector.

There has also been a tendency to present a picture of a dual Irish economy in the pre-Famine period, with a small commercial economy found along the east and south coast in the vicinity of cities and ports such as Dublin, Cork or Waterford, and a much larger subsistence economy which was characteristic of the rest of Ireland and especially of the western seaboard.[12] In fact the available

data concerning Irish agricultural exports belie this impression. Indeed in the decades immediately before the Famine there is evidence that grain exports from ports in counties Mayo and Sligo were expanding rapidly and that a new export trade in eggs was developing from western ports.[13] This expansion of trade was largely a consequence of better communications.

In 1812, as Austin Bourke has noted, it was simply impossible to transport grain to market in north Mayo, because there were no roads in the area.[14] As K.H. Connell pointed out, poteen distillation was one logical response to this problem; it made oats much more portable, and indeed potable; it also added value, though there was a certain loss in income for the revenue commissioners.[15] By the eve of the Famine however, the road networks in most western areas had improved remarkably, largely because of the relief works programmes carried out by the Commissioners of Public Works and their predecessors. By 1841 the only parts of Ireland which were more than ten miles from public transport were the Erris and Achill areas of Mayo, Gweedore and adjoining areas in Donegal and some other tiny areas in Donegal, Kerry and Cork.[16]

Was this growth in agricultural exports a good or a bad thing? The evidence is mixed. The export trade in eggs from Co. Mayo for example, only seems to have developed following the collapse in domestic linen spinning[17] and some of the eggs which ended up on English breakfast tables would presumably otherwise have been eaten in the west of Ireland. Austin Bourke associates the growth of grain exports with an increasing reliance on the low-grade lumper potato and an overall deterioration in the Irish diet.[18]

There is some truth in Bourke's argument, but it is equally clear that the Irish population, which rose from 5 million or so in 1800 to over 8 million in 1841, could not have been fed without a substantial increase in agricultural output and there is clear evidence that agricultural exports were rising at the same time. Ó Gráda suggests that agricultural output rose by approximately 80 per cent between 1800 and 1845.[19] This was achieved by a variety of mechanisms.

There was a considerable expansion in the amount of cultivated land, as waste land was cleared and planted, though it is difficult to be precise about the actual growth of cultivated acreage.[20] Land already in cultivation was drained and improved. The sickle made way for the scythe, an innovation which permitted a much larger area to be cut by one man in a day and one which also cut the crops more effectively. Less grain was left for the gleaners or the birds.

In western areas where rundale holdings were dominant, there are numerous contemporary descriptions of holdings being squared and organised into individual farms - this is generally regarded as an essential first step towards modernising agricultural practices. [21]

Breeds of cattle such as Ayreshires, Herefords and Shorthorns began to supplant traditional Irish breeds such as the Kerry cow. At some stage between the late 1820s and the early 1840s, according to John O'Donovan, the Shorthorn became Ireland's premier breed. Some large farmers were also beginning to feed cattle on turnips and mangel wurzels during winter months.[22] Landlords provided premium bulls for their tenantry and established farming societies and some of these in turn organised ploughing matches, which were used to promote the merits of iron ploughs.[23]

Between the 1820s and the early 1840s, the Shorthorn became Ireland's premier breed.

There are innumerable descriptions of agricultural improvements and improvers in Ireland from the time of Arthur Young until the Famine and for much of this period there was also an active agricultural press in the form of the *Irish Farmers' Gazette*. If descriptions of premium bulls, agricultural shows and the innovations of improving farmers were the only source available to us concering Irish agriculture during these years, it would be easy

Landlords established farming societies and some of these in turn organised ploughing matches, although on a smaller scale than that held near London in 1842 and featured in the Illustrated London News.

to conclude that Ireland before the Famine had indeed achieved the status of a modern agricultural economy. Against this we can of course weigh the equally-numerous accounts of poverty and backwardness provided by sources such as the Poor Inquiry or the Devon Commission, which prompts the question: how much impact did these improvements have on ordinary farmers? And, perhaps how do you define an ordinary farmer?

Again it is difficult to know. One Cork landlord told the Devon Commission that the local farming society had made scant impact on working farmers, though it had been responsible for introducing iron swing ploughs to the area.[24] Alexander Somerville, a Scottish journalist who toured Ireland during the Famine years, was sufficiently perceptive to notice that agricultural improvements of this ilk, i.e. involving capital investment, were often associated with complex religious and cultural questions. In a letter from Roscommon dated 24th February 1847 he wrote about Mr James Clapperton, steward of the Ballinasloe Agricultural Society. Clapperton, a farmer's son from Tweedside in Scotland was agent to

Lord Clancarty and an enthusiast for all forms of agricultural improvement.

According to Alexander Somerville he had already enabled some of Lord Clancarty's tenants "to double, triple and quadruple their produce, by introducing among them a superior style of cultivation". So far so good. Somerville continues:

> Unfortunately, however, Lord Clancarty looks to improved agriculture as a means of church proselytism. He mingles the produce of the farm-yard and the Thirty-nine Articles together, the stall feeding of cattle and attendance at the Protestant church, the instruction on thorough drainage and the instruction in the church catechism. A new dwelling-house, or barn, or stable, or road is equivalent on his estate to a new religion. The use of a bull of improved breed is associated with a renunciation of the bulls of Rome.[25]

As this quotation reveals, most aspects of Irish history have political and cultural dimensions, even stall feeding of cattle. While it is important to note that pre-Famine Ireland appears to have been fully aware of the various agricultural improvements which would appeal to agricultural experts from Britain, most of the increase in agricultural output before the Famine was achieved by less glamorous methods, methods which relied less on modern swing ploughs than on the spade and on back-breaking toil. It relied particularly on using large quantities of labour to clear fields of stones, carry seaweed from the shore - the new roads could facilitate this - and to collect animal manure.[26]

Labour and productivity

The quantities of labour used in pre-Famine agriculture are almost beyond our comprehension. Sir Charles Coote's RDS survey of Co. Cavan wrote of 12 men being required to turn the sods as part of the process of sowing potatoes in lazy beds. Almost as an afterthought he noted that women and children would precede the men with seed.[27] Four or five haymakers were expected to follow each scytheman.[28] According to an account given by Edward

Wakefield in 1812, one farmer in Grange, Co. Tipperary hired 42 men to dig an acre for potatoes; 12 girls and 8 boys to plant it; 12 men to shovel it; 12 women to weed it and 38 men to dig out the potatoes, and presumably an unspecified number of additional women and boys to lift them.[29] Such accounts can be multiplied for every conceivable form of tillage; indeed flax seems to have been the most labour-intensive crop of all.

All the above descriptions relate to state-of-the-art modern commercial farms, not to the so-called primitive subsistence economy, though both sectors would appear to have had more in common than is often realised: both are highly labour intensive, the difference being mainly one of scale. It is also important to note that both commercial agriculture and the small holdings occupied by cottiers were heavily intertwined. The 42 men digging the field in Grange, Co. Tipperary were probably cottiers, who although paid nominally in wages were in practice paid in land - conacre land which they used to grow potatoes. On many commercial farms the conacre plots given to cottiers were moved from year to year and the potatoes which formed the cottiers' wage and his food were actually part of the crop rotation on the larger farm.

Although Connacht was the province with the highest percentage of farms between 1 and 5 acres in size, (64.4 per cent), holdings of less than one acre were most common in Leinster, where they account for almost one in four (22.5 per cent) of all holdings. These small plots were occupied by cottiers.[30] While there was considerable seasonal unemployment in pre-Famine Ireland, for much of the year, when the weather permitted, this was a hard-working labour force. Trevelyan did not realise that the cottiers who only needed five weeks to plant and harvest potatoes and to save the family's turf were working for a commercial farmer for the remainder of the year - to pay off the rent of their potato plot. In many instances, as O'Neill argues, adult male labourers were fully occupied on larger holdings, with the result that women and children were forced to carry out most of the work on the cottier plot.[31]

Although the relationship between large and small holdings, or between subsistence plots and commercial farms was less evident in more peripheral parts of Ireland, it did exist. Migratory labourers, the spailpini fanach, moved from areas such as Kerry into Cork and Tipperary; harvest workers came from Monaghan and Cavan into Meath. The high rate of population increase in pre-Famine Ireland meant that labour was freely available in very large quantities for very little money. One reason why labour was so cheap was because it could be fed so cheaply: the ultimate subsistence wage, after all, is what it will take to keep a labourer alive and capable of doing his or her work. Thanks to the potato the Irish subsistence wage was extremely low.

The potato was a wonder crop, the only subsistence foodstuff which provides a nearly-perfect diet, a crop which would feed a family on very little land, in almost all types of Irish soil, irrespective of rain or lack of sunshine. So all of Irish farming, even the most modern and most commercial holdings, rested ultimately on the potato - if only because it ensured a regular supply of cheap labour.

The final question which I shall pose, but not answer, about the pre-Famine agricultural labour force is, how hard did they work? Several accounts at the time, notably the comments of a leading Irishman, Sir Robert Kane, suggest that so many workers were needed because productivity per worker was low. While many foreign commentators linked low agricultural output to cultural factors - Irish labourers taking time out to dance, make music, talk or celebrate, Kane blamed it on bad food. He argued that English labourers, whose wages were double those in Ireland, "would not cost the employer more".[32]

Labour was used more efficiently in England and probably in lowland Scotland, but most Irish labourers had two jobs to carry out. They had to work for a farmer, and to care for their conacre plot and probably to save their own turf. Insofar as labour productivity was lower in Ireland than in Britain, this is more likely to be accounted for by lack of capital rather than by laziness.[33]

The potato blight and the consequent Famine transformed this situation overnight. In the first place, Irish agriculture could no longer feed the Irish population: in a normal year the potato accounted for approximately two-thirds of the vegetable foodstuff produced in the country, e.g. potatoes plus all forms of grain for both human and animal consumption.[34] Once the potato crop was destroyed, there was insufficient food available in Ireland, even if all food exports had ceased. The country consequently became heavily dependent on imports for its survival.

The blight also destroyed a complete socio-economic system. Many cottiers who had worked for larger farmers in return for conacre often abandoned their work to seek employment on public works. This was quite a logical response: they were paid in land, so if the conacre plot now consisted of blighted potatoes, why continue to rent it when a family needed immediate food? During the 1846-47 season, the Famine undoubtedly reduced the supply of both labour and horses available on Irish farms. By March 1847, over 700,000 labourers were employed on public works; no sector of the economy could afford such a loss of labour, unless you believe Trevelyan's picture of an Irish labouring population which was out of work for most of the year. Farmers' sons and farmers also went in search of work, sometimes motivated by sheer greed, but often because they too needed the cash to buy food and farmers often dispensed with labourers because they could no longer afford to feed them.

One Board of Works official based in Co. Cavan noted that "the high price of food not only itself aggravates it (distress) but compels farmers, who formerly used to give 4d a day and food, to discharge their labour".[35] Despite the many complaints about the low wages paid on relief works, they were considerably higher than the regular daily wage paid by most farmers, so farmers who wished to keep labour had to pay higher wages, at a time when the price of food and the burden of poor rates were both rising.

Farmhorses were much in demand, both to work on relief schemes, where they could earn much more than a labourer, particularly if accompanied by a cart, and to transport food - not out of Ireland as John Mitchel and other writers have alleged - but into parts of Ireland which were normally almost self-sufficient in food and consequently had no regular freight transport systems.[36] Many accounts written by men who travelled throughout Ireland during the autumn and winter of 1846-47 refer to the lack of work being carried out in the fields. In October 1846, Lt. Col. Jones, a Board of Works inspector, wrote from Newry:

> The weather has been favourable; and the ground in a good state and not a single plough have I seen at work or any land being turned up by hand labour; all the land of the country appears to be laying fallow. The fields have the appearance of being deserted.

Another account written from Co. Waterford early in 1847 noted that the only people to be seen ploughing in the fields were farmers' sons, all the labourers had been dismissed because farmers could not afford to feed them.[37] Many small farmers were unable to sow crops because they had been forced either to eat or sell their seed.[38] For larger farmers, particularly those with a large acreage of grain, the higher cost of labour was more than offset by escalating grain prices. The price of oats in 1846 was more than 50 per cent higher than in the previous year[39] and there are so many references to farmers holding grain off the market in the autumn of 1846, in the hope that prices would rise even further, that they cannot be discounted.

Alexander Somerville gives a graphic description of the panic among farmers in the Carlow area in late January 1847 when the price of wheat and oats fell by approximately five shillings a quarter: "every farmer offered to sell, but the millers would not buy, in hopes of forcing them still further into the panic."[40] Bearing that in mind, we should perhaps consider how Irish farmers would have reacted if the British government had attempted to ban exports, or to otherwise control the price of grain, as many critiques of its policy have recommended.[41]

The tendency for Irish farmers to dismiss their labourers was not a short-term phenomenon. Repeated attacks of blight destroyed any prospect of rebuilding a conacre/potato economy. The 1847 Poor Law Extension Act left Irish ratepayers carrying the full cost of Famine and poor relief, with each electoral district responsible for supporting its own poor; this increased the pressures on the larger farmers to dispense with labourers.[42] Landlords were responsible for all poor rates on holdings valued at £4 or less, so they became extremely eager to rid themselves of small farmers. The outcome was a massive series of clearances and the highest eviction levels ever seen in Ireland. Evictions peaked at almost 20,000 families in 1850 - over 100,000 persons.[43] More families were undoubtedly evicted during the late 1840s and early 1850s than throughout the remainder of the nineteenth century. In 1847 there were almost 730,000 farms in Ireland; by 1851 the number had fallen to 570,000.[44]

Although all the "missing" farms apparently had less than 15 acres, the Famine also took its toll on some of the larger farmers. The worst affected were probably larger farmers living in the poorest areas such as Mayo, west Galway or other parts of Connacht and west Munster. Poor rates reached such impossibly high levels in some of these areas that some larger farmers simply packed up and left. There are numerous reports in 1849 of larger farmers selling their cattle and belongings and buying passage to

America for all the family[45] - which would have been quite an expensive proposition. The impact in Mayo was such that some people argued that some communities seem to have lost their potential leaders.[46] The timing of these reports is noteworthy; by 1849 such farmers would have faced five years of record rates bills, with no apparent end in sight.

For those that remained there is evidence of a change of direction. The mid 1840s not only brought the Famine. The repeal of the Corn Laws in the summer of 1846 heralded an end to artificially-high grain prices, though grain prices remained quite high in the early 1850s. Farmers were more immediately affected by the sharp rise in the real cost of labour. Wages increased because potato yields dropped and potatoes were more expensive. As a result labourers were now more dependent on cash to buy shop food and more inclined to demand tea with their meals.[47]

The shift to grazing

Higher labour costs and the prospect of lower grain prices suggested that farmers should shift from tillage to grazing. Crotty argued that the shift out of tillage into cattle farming started in the years 1815-45, but data on agricultural output do not lend his argument much support.[48] Some farmers may have wished to make this change before the Famine; in many cases they may have been deterred from doing so by the threat of agrarian violence carried out by secret societies. The list of murder victims in Co. Tipperary in the decade or so prior to the Famine is heavily dominated by farmers and land agents who were intent on consolidating holdings in order to switch into cattle. [49] However, the shift to cattle farming appears to have begun in earnest during the Famine years.

Beef and cattle prices were relatively stable, indeed many smaller farmers were probably forced to sell cattle to feed their families and impoverished workers were buying less meat. The agricultural statistics suggest that the number of cattle on farms of 30 acres or more rose by 25 per cent between 1847 and 1850 [50] - though part of this apparent increase may be due to more thorough work by the RIC men who carried out the agricultural census.[51] However by the late 1850s the trend was conclusive: cattle prices were buoyant, grain prices were not and labour costs showed no signs of declining. The appalling weather conditions in the early 1860s provided a final nail in the coffin for many grain farmers.[52]

Whether the shift from tillage to cattle was good or bad for Irish agriculture is a moot point. It meant a long-term reduction in labour demand and it also brought the long-term survival of many small farms into question, because a farmer who concentrated on grazing needed a much larger holding to survive than one who was predominantly engaged in tillage.

The trend towards grazing was inevitable in the long-term, given the repeal of the Corn Laws and the rapid expansion in grain exports from the New World. If the Famine had not occurred the transformation might possibly have been delayed, or might have occurred at a more gradual pace.[53] The Famine was undoubtedly bad for many aspects of Irish agriculture. Agricultural statistics suggest that yields of potatoes, oats, wheat, barley and flax all fell in the decade or more following the Famine. The 1847 yield per acre of potatoes - admittedly achieved on a very small acreage - was not exceeded until 1929. This drop in yields appears to have been a consequence of less intensive methods of cultivation and particularly of less intensive manuring.

In the case of the potato, the apparently long term drop in yields also reflects the impact of potato blight. As labour costs rose in post-Famine Ireland farmers cut corners: ploughs replaced the spade, less time was spent hauling manure or seaweed and spreading it on the land; attention to detail lapsed. In time Irish farming was mechanised and it adapted to changing circumstances, but the subsequent rise in yields was invariably accompanied by a steady fall in acreage.[54]

The trends in crop yields suggest that the teeming masses of pre-Famine labourers were not nearly as superfluous as many so-called experts at the time had suggested. This is borne out by data on agricultural output. By 1854, when the immediate impact of Famine had gone, Irish agriculture was apparently producing 16 per cent less than in 1845, with 25 per cent fewer workers.[55] (This in fact may understate the fall in output). So total output had declined though output per head had increased. This in fact became the trend during much of the succeeding half century: higher output per head, but a fall in total ouput: a smaller cake, but fewer people to share it. So what conclusions should we draw? It is necessary to keep a balance. If pre-Famine agriculture produced more food and functioned more efficiently than it has often been credited with doing, this was achieved at the cost of an extremely low standard of living and it would be naive to assume that Irish labourers would have been content to subsist at such low standards for the remainder of the nineteenth century. The beginning of mass emigration, which was already well established on the eve of the Famine, suggests otherwise.

Nevertheless the shock which the Famine administered to Irish farming was not a good thing: the blight crippled the country's staple diet and that alone was a very serious matter. Given that the potato underpinned most of pre-Famine farming, the repercussions were almost endless. It would have been difficult for any economy or economic sector to adjust overnight to a shock of this scale. If the Famine years cleared out a lot of the pre-Famine structure, in many ways it did not do a sufficiently thorough job. Smallholdings survived, particularly in western areas, which could not be viable without a flourishing potato crop; yet because of the potato blight these small farmers were now less capable of producing the higher living standards which Irish people were beginning to seek.

Finally the emotional images which remained, of a pre-Famine rural economy based on small tillage holdings, combined with a high population density, continued to haunt politicians, farmers and those interested in rural Ireland in what I suspect was a baleful manner. Much of the agricultural policy of twentieth century Ireland has been an attempt to recreate or shore up the residues of pre-Famine Ireland, long after the blight had doomed them to extinction. ▩

References

1. Jonathan Pim, (1847). *Observations on the evils resulting to Ireland from the insecurity of title and the existing laws of real property; with some Suggestions towards a Remedy.* (Dublin).
2. Cited in N. Mansergh, (1965). *The Irish Question, 1840-1921.* of J.L. Mc Cracken, Belfast, p. 126; J.O Donovan, (1940), *An Economic History of Livestock in Ireland,* (Cork), pp 167- 79
3. Alexis de Tocqueville, (1835). *Journey in Ireland. July-August 1835.* Translated and edited by Emmet Larkin, (Washington 1990) pp 112-3.
4. Sir Charles Trevelyan,(1850). *The Irish crisis* (London), p. 4.
5. P.M.A. Bourke, (1993). "The visitation of God'? The role of the potato on the eve of the famine", in Austin Bourke, *'The visitation of God'? The potato and the great Irish famine,* Jacqueline Hill and Cormac Ó Gráda eds. (Dublin), p. 66.
6. Eric Almquist, (1977). "Mayo and beyond: land, domestic industry, and rural transformation in the Irish west 1750-1900" . Ph.D. Boston University, pp 173-5; James S. Donnelly, *The land and the people of nineteenth-century Cork. The rural economy and the land question* (London, 1975), pp 30-1. Bourke "Towards the precipice" in *'The visitiation of God', The Potato and the Great Irish Famine* (eds. Hill, and Ó Gráda,) Dublin p. 12.
7. Peter Solar, (1983). "Agricultural productivity and Economic Development in Ireland and Scotland in the early 19th Century. In: *Ireland and Scotland, 1600 - 1850* (eds. Devine, T.M. and Dickson, D.), p. 81.
8. Cormac Ó Gráda, (1989). "Poverty, population and agriculture", in W. J Vaughan, (ed), *A new history of Ireland V. Ireland under the Union part I 1801-70* (Oxford), p. 123.
9. Solar, "Agricultural productivity", p. 76.
10. J.S. Donnelly (1975). *Cork,* p. 32.
11. Solar, (1979). "The agricultural trade statistics in the Irish railway commissioners report", in *Irish economic and social history,* vi, , p. 35.
12. P. Lynch, and J. Vaizey, (1960). *Guinness's brewery in the Irish economy, 1759-1876,* (Cambridge) chapter 1.
13. Solar, (1979). "Agricultural trade statistics". p. 35.
14. Bourke, (1993). "Towards the precipice: the potato in pre-famine Ireland", in *The visitation of God'?* p. 23.
15. K.H. Connell, (1968). "Illicit distillation in Ireland"in K.H. Connell, *Irish peasant society. Four historical essays.* (Oxford).
16. T. W. Freeman, (1957). *Pre-famine Ireland,* (Manchester), p. 112.
17. E.Almquist, (1977). "Mayo and beyond", pp 253-4.
18. A. Bourke, (1993). "Towards the precipice",in *The visitation of God'?* p. 23.
19. C. Ó Gráda, (1989). "Poverty, population and agriculture, 1801-45" in W.J. Vaughan (ed), *A new history of Ireland, V. Ireland under the union. Part I 1801-70.* (Oxford) p. 127.
20. K.H. Connell, (1950). "The colonization of waste land in Ireland, 1780-1845", *Economic history review,* iiii no. 7 (195)), pp 44-71; P.M.A. Bourke, "The agricultural statistics of the 1841 census of lIreland, a critical review", in *'Visitation of God',* pp 74-89.
21. D. Mc Court, (1981). "The decline of rundale" in Peter Roebuck (ed), *Planatation to partition. Essays in Ulster history in honour of J.L. McCracken,* (Belfast, 1981), p. 126.

22. J. O'Donovan, (1940). *An Economic History of Livestock in Ireland*, (Cork), pp 167-79.
23. J.S. Donnelly. (1975). *The Land and the People of 19th Century Cork*. (London), p. 37; Greig, W. (1976). *General Report on the Gosford Estates in County Armagh*, 1821. (Belfast), pp 182-183.
24. Donnelly, (1975). p. 37.
25. Alexander Somerville, (1994). *Letters from Ireland during the Famine of 1847* (ed. Snell, D.K.M.), Dublin, pp. 76-77.
26. For a discussion of the importance of manuring see McGregor, P. (1980). The impact of the blight on the pre-Famine rural economy of Ireland. *Economic and Social Review* 15: No. 4, pp. 289-303
27. Quoted in K. O'Neill, (1984). *Family and Farm in Pre-Famine Ireland: The Parish of Killeshandra* (Madison, Wisconsin), p. 87.
28. J. Bell, and M. Watson, (1986). *Irish Farming 1750-1900.*(Edinburgh), p. 143.
29. E. Wakefield, (1812). *An Account of Ireland, Statistical and Political.* (London), 2 volumes , i, p. 449.
30. Joel Mokyr, (1983). *Why Ireland Starved* (London), p. 19.
31. K. O'Neill, (1984)."Family and Farm": pp.103-105.
32. Mokyr, (1983). *Why Ireland Starved* (London), pp. 218-21.
33. Solar, (1983). "Agricultural Productivity:" In: *Ireland and Scotland, 1600-1850*, Edinburgh.
34. Solar, (1989). Calculates that in 1845 potatoes accounted for 23 kcal/day of Irish domestic production, a total net of seed of 34.3 kcal. The great famine was no ordinary subsistence crisis. In: *Famine: the Irish Experience , 900-1900: Subsistence Crises and Famine in Ireland* (ed. Crawford, E.M.),(Edinburgh, 1989), p. 123.
35. Quoted in Mary Daly, (1986). *The Famine in Ireland* (Dublin), p. 64.
36. Somerville, (1994). *Letters from Ireland*, p.39
37. Daly, (1986). *The Famine in Ireland* (Dublin), p. 64.
38. Somerville, (1994). *Letters from Ireland*, p.147.
39. Daly, (1986). *The Famine in Ireland* (Dublin), p. 58.
40. Somerville, (1994). *Letters from Ireland,* (Dublin), p.34.
41. Christine Kinealy, (1994). *This Great Calamity* (Dublin), p. 89.
42. Kinealy, (1994). *This Great Calamity* (Dublin), pp 181-183.
43. J.S. Donnelly, Landlords and Tenants. In: *New History* (ed. Vaughan) p. 338.
44. Bourke, (1993). Agricultural Statistics. In: *The Visitation of God.* p.76.
45. O. MacDonagh, (1956). Irish Emigration to the United States of America and the British Colonies during the Famine. In: *The Great Famine* (eds. Edwards, R.E. and Williams, T. W.) (Dublin), pp. 320-321 and p. 331.
46. D. McCabe,(1991). Law, Conflict and Social Order: County Mayo, 1820-1845. *Ph.D. Thesis*. University College Dublin, p. 30.
47. *Sixth Report of the Medical Office of the Privy Council.* Appendix 6. Report by Dr. E. Smith on the food of the labouring classes in England, pp. 282-329.

48. R. Crotty, (1966). *Irish Agricultural Production: its Volume and Structure,* (Cork), Chapter 2; Ó Gráda, C. In: *New History* (ed. Vaughan), p. 123.
49. M. Beames, (1985). *Peasants and Power: the Whiteboy Movement and their Control in Pre-Famine Ireland* (Brighton), p.18.
50. M.E. Daly, (1986). *The Famine in Ireland* (Dublin), p. 65.
51. C. Ó Gráda, (1994). *Ireland: A New Economic History,* 1780-1939 (Oxford) p.114.
52. J.S. Donnelly, (1976). The Irish Agricultural Depression, 1859-64. *Irish Economic and Social History* 3: 33-54.
53. K. O Rourke, (1991). Did the Great Famine Matter. *Journal of Economic History* 51: 1-22.
54. A. Bourke, The Average Yield of Food Crops in Ireland on the Eve of the Great Famine. In: *'The Visitation of God'?* pp.151-154.
55. C. Ó Gráda, 1984. Irish Agricultural Output before and after the Famine. *Journal of European Economic History* (Spring), pp. 151-154.

THE POTATO AND LATE BLIGHT IN IRELAND

Leslie J. Dowley

Origin of the potato

The natives of South America were the first to discover the delights of this historic tuber and benefit from its incredible productivity. From archaeological records, Salaman[1] states that the potato was brought into cultivation about 2,000 years before the Spanish conquest. However, more recent evidence from carbon dating has shown that the potato was present in South America as far back as 11,000 BC. and is therefore as ancient as the cereals of the 'Old World'. [2] While potatoes have been growing in South America for at least 13,000 years, they have only been cultivated from about 8,000 BC. It is now generally recognised that the centre of origin or genetic diversity of the potato is located near lake Titicaca on the Peru/Bolivian border.

Centre of origin of the potato

The potato belongs to the *Solanaceae* family and is botanically related to tomato, tobacco, eggplant, pepper, petunia and the deadly nightshade. The tuber bearing species belong to the genus *Solanum* and are mainly autotetraploids. However, most of the species within this genus are non-tuber bearing and can be found in many different ploidy levels. These ploidy levels vary from 2n = 24 to 2n = 72. Today most of the South American varieties grown belong to the species *Solanum andegenum* where 2n = 48 while in Europe they belong to the closely related *S. tuberosum*. It is felt by Salaman that *Solanum stenotomum* (2n = 24) is the original ancestor which gave rise to *S. andegenum* by natural chromosome doubling.

Davidson[3] was of the opinion that the 48 chromosome (or tetraploid) potatoes now grown in Europe have originated mainly from Chile and not from the north-western part of South America as originally believed. This conclusion was probably influenced by the findings of the Russian botanical team of Vavilov, Bukasov and Jujepczuk who carried out a comprehensive study of the species in South America from 1925 to 1933 and concluded that the first introduction was of *S. tuberosum* from Chile.

Even at that time the Russian team did concede the close relationship between *S. tuberosum* and *S. andegenum* which was associated with the more northerly areas of South America. However, Salaman disputes this theory stating that it was unlikely, if not impossible, that viable tubers could have reached Europe from Chile at that time. In Salaman's opinion, it is much more likely that the initial tubers brought to Europe were of the Andean type (*S. andegenum*) and probably originated in Colombia. They may have been exported through the port of Cartegena.

It is now known that breeding within the *S. andegenum* group can produce progeny of the *S. tuberosum* group, especially when the progeny are selected under long daylength conditions. This lends considerable support to Salaman's theory.

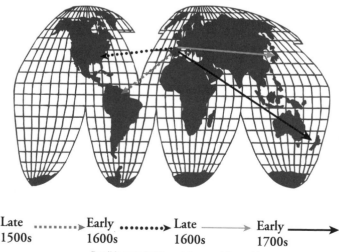

Late	Early	Late	Early
1500s	1600s	1600s	1700s

Possible spread of the potato around the world.

The spread of the potato to Europe

The first European connection with the South American potato is attributed to the Spanish soldier, Pedro de Cieza de Leon, who came across the tuber in the Upper Cauca Valley of Colombia in 1538. However, according to Bourke[4] it did not reach Spain until 1565. Salaman records that it was served to Europeans in a Seville hospital in 1573 and perhaps earlier. While Davidson puts the first introduction to Europe as 1588, the current thinking would seem to favour the earlier date of introduction.

From Spain the tubers were transported by Catholic monks to Italy and from there to Belgium and the rest of Europe by the Papal Legates. The potato was introduced to China and Japan in the seventeenth century and New Zealand in the eighteenth century. To reach North America the potato travelled back across the Atlantic from Europe and appears to have been grown first in Virginia where it was recorded in 1620 and in Pennsylvania in 1685.[5]

While the identity of the individual who was first responsible for bringing this important food source to Europe is still unclear, the whole subject seems to be surrounded by legend, mystery and tradition. What is clear is that the original import to Europe was not of a single variety as we understand the term today but as a mixture of genetic lines. It is also possible that a number of imports took place around the same time or that true seed may have been the original source of the plant.

Introduction of the potato to Ireland

By the middle of the seventeenth century one can find many references to the potato as a source of food for the Irish. This would suggest, that even by that time, the potato was extensively grown in Ireland. However, it cannot be established with any degree of certainty when the potato was introduced to Ireland, or by whom, but it is stated by Bourke to have been sometime within the last 15 years of the sixteenth century. This would mean that the potato has now been grown in Ireland for some 400 years.

Many different theories of how the potato was introduced to Ireland have been investigated by Davidson, Salaman, Bourke and others.

One theory attributes the introduction of the potato to Sir Francis Drake, who spent two years hiding in 'Drakes Pool' outside Crosshaven, Co. Cork on his return from South America.[6] It is known that Drake first came across the potato on 28th November, 1577 on the Isle of Mocha off the coast of Chile, but it is not clear what interest he took in this new food source at that time. However, it is known that at a later date Drake took potatoes on board at Cartegena as a food source for his crew. He left Cartegena on the 30th March, 1586 and arrived in Plymouth on the 26th of July, a little late, but in time to have planted any remaining tubers.[7]

The second and most widely accepted theory attributes the introduction to Sir Walter Raleigh who is said to have brought the root from Virginia. Davidson considers this to be highly unlikely as Raleigh was never in Virginia, where the crop was unknown at that time, and of his five expeditions only one touched on Ireland (Smerwick, Co. Kerry) and the crew were in a state of semi-starvation.

Other unsubstantiated reports suggest that the potato was first introduced to Youghal by Sir Walter Raleigh. Raleigh did have a large estate in the area and was Mayor of Youghal from 1588 to 1599 around the time the potato was first introduced. It is also apparent that the cultivation of the potato was well understood in that area at an early stage, indicating that the potato may have been introduced to Cork earlier than in many other areas.

While Davidson seems to discount the Raleigh theory, Salaman gives it a little more credence. His belief in the Raleigh theory seems to be centred firstly on the fact that Heriot (Raleigh's agent) is stated to have received tubers from Drake's ship which left Cartegena on 30th March. There is also a statement by Robert Southwell that his grandfather, Sir Robert Southwell, who obtained tubers from Sir Walter Raleigh, was the first person to bring the root to Ireland. If this is true, then the introduction to Ireland could also have been in 1586.

There was also a belief that the potato had come directly from Spain to Ireland. This theory may have had some credibility in that there was a flourishing trade between the two countries at that time, and about 1740 there was a reference to the potato as An Spaineach Geal or the White Spaniard.[8] It is also attributed to a shipwreck off the Galway coast associated with the Spanish Armada in 1588.

The potato is botanically related to the tomato, tobacco, eggplant, pepper, petunia and the deadly nightshade.

Progress of the potato in Ireland

According to Bourke the potato was first introduced to Ireland sometime in the last 15 years of the sixteenth century. This would accommodate the theory of Raleigh or Southwell being the introducers in 1586.

Seventeenth Century: The lack of reliable census data prior to 1841 makes it difficult to trace changes in the population prior to that date or to accurately determine the acreage of potatoes grown at any stage. However, it seems to be generally agreed that the potato found a very agreeable home in Ireland and its cultivation and use spread rapidly. Salaman argues that due to the widespread devastation and misery which prevailed at the end of the sixteenth century, there was not the normal prejudice which one would expect towards a new food crop. The crop was also free from disease, easy to grow, easy to conserve, highly productive, pleasing to the palate and required the minimum of cultivation and capital inputs while at the same time producing its own seed for the following crop.

Bourke also related the suitable meteorological conditions (wet and overcast) to the general acceptability of the potato in Ireland.

The first official record of the potato in Ireland is to be found in the Montgomery Manuscripts which refer to potatoes being grown in Co. Down in 1606. If the potato, as is suggested, made its initial appearance in the south, it must have been rapidly adopted as a source of food to have reached the north some 20 years later. The council book of Youghal Corporation records that there was a toll on potatoes (roots) as early as 1623, again indicating that the potato had a level of general cultivation at an early stage.[9]

Bourke states that between 1570 and 1675 the potato became a supplementary food and a standby against famine. According to Salaman this factor saved Ireland in the winter of 1629-30 when there was a dearth in England and again during the Cromwellian war of 1645-52. As early as 1659 Robert Boyle had plans for experiments with potatoes to determine the effect of seed cutting on productivity and composts on quality.[10] In 1663 Robert Boyle's gardener sent him a box of potatoes from his estate in Lismore, Co. Waterford for distribution to his friends in the Royal Society in England. The tubers were accompanied by a letter giving details as to the proper husbandry to adopt which indicated that the husbandry of the crop was well advanced in that area by the middle of the sixteenth century.

The Irish also developed the "lazy bed" system of growing potatoes during this period which was similar to some of the production systems in the Andes. The 'lazy bed' system had distinct advantages in wet and poorly drained soils and was also used for over-wintering the produce. All the cultivation was done by hand with a spade referred to as a 'loy' or 'fack' which was very similar to the Peruvian 'taclla'. Salaman alludes to the similarities between the two cultural systems but suggests that these came about by adopting similar solutions to identical problems rather than by a transfer of culture. Manure was provided by the farm animals and in some cases seaweed was also used.

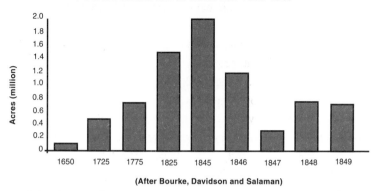

POTATO ACREAGE IN IRELAND 1650-1849

(After Bourke, Davidson and Salaman)

John Forster of Buckinghamshire, in a pamphlet dealing exclusively with the potato, was the first to refer to the potato as the 'Irish Potato' in 1664 and this term is still in use in many parts of the world.

Eighteenth Century: Ireland experienced the 'Penal Laws' together with trade restrictions during the first 75 years of the eighteenth century. These led to the collapse of many industries and a general deterioration in economic activity. This was coupled with insecurity of land tenure, rack renting, absentee landlords and the sub-division of small holdings. All these factors induced a nationwide state of poverty and discontent which in turn led to greater dependence on the potato. For the first half of the century the potato was the winter food for the poor. However, over the next 50 years it became the staple food of all small farmers and cottiers for most of the year.[11]

Salaman records seven general failures of the potato crop during the century. These were attributed mainly to unfavourable weather conditions, such as the first and most serious failure in 1739, which was caused by severe frost. During this failure it is said that 300,000 people lost their lives (see paper by David Dickson). During the century the potato appears to have remained free from disease problems until 1769. In that year we see the first general failure attributed to a pathogen. This was referred to at the time as 'curl', we now know that it was due to potato leaf roll virus.

During this century there seems to be scant reference to any improvements in the husbandry of the crop, but potato breeding appears to have been widely practised. According to Davidson a number of famous varieties such as the Black Potato (pre 1730), the Apple (1768), the Cup and the Lumper (pre 1808) were all introduced during this period.

Nineteenth Century: The rapid rise in the population of the country in the late eighteenth and early nineteenth centuries was accompanied by an expansion of the area under potatoes and the use of very marginal land for this purpose. The early part of the century can be characterised by the almost complete dependence of the majority of the population on a single crop for their existence. As we approach the Famine period, this dependency increased if anything and the better quality potato varieties were gradually replaced by the higher yielding, poor quality variety, Lumper.

Market day in Dublin - 1843.

Apart from its use as a human food the potato also found favour as animal feed, especially for pigs. In large parts of the country this dependence was on a single variety - Lumper. The inherent dangers of such a complete dependence were not frequently alluded to. However, there were warnings from the Select Committee for the Advances of Public Works in 1835 and again by a Captain Chad in 1839.[12]

From the early part of the century up to the Famine there were eight general failures of the potato crop in Ireland.[13] While three of these were attributed to the weather the remainder were attributed to pathogenic organisms such as *Fusarium, Botrytis* and *Erwinia*. This is the first time that bacteria and fungi seem to have been associated with crop failures. After the Famine there were two general failures which were both attributed to late blight.

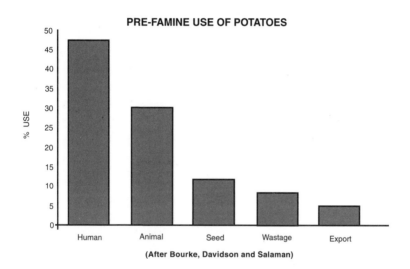

PRE-FAMINE USE OF POTATOES

(After Bourke, Davidson and Salaman)

The Famine period

The Famine of 1845-1849 was caused by a fungal disease which led to the failure of the potato crop. According to Bourke the first record of the disease in Ireland was on 6th September, 1845 in the *Waterford Freeman* and the *Dublin Evening Post*. However, it has since been confirmed by Nelson[14] that it was observed by Dr David Moore in the Botanic Gardens in Dublin as early as 20th August, 1845.

Dr David Moore,
National Botanic Gardens, Dublin.

1845: In Ireland, the late arrival of the disease and its irregular spread during 1845 meant that the loss in production was relatively small. The main loss was caused by the subsequent rotting of the tubers before and after harvest. Bourke estimates the loss to have been 40 per cent due to rotting tubers but because of the exceptional yields of that year the shortfall in production was between 25 and 30 per cent that of normal.

1846: The partial failure in 1845 and the subsequent rotting of the stored tubers resulted in severe hardship but not famine conditions at the beginning of 1846. The shortage of seed tubers also resulted in a reduction in the area planted.

In 1846 the disease arrived earlier and the whole potato crop was destroyed by early August, when tuber production had just started in the late maincrop varieties. As a result the entire food source for most of the population was wiped out.

There followed the most intense period of 'The Great Hunger' which saw the intensification of evictions, the introduction of the relief works, importation of maize from the USA, soup kitchens, workhouses and charitable donations administered by the Quakers as well as the establishment of the Relief Commission.

1847: The almost complete loss of the 1846 crop had its worst effects in the early part of "Black '47". Apart from famine, the lack of food led to diseases such as scurvy, vitamin B deficiency, dysentery, typhus and cholera (see Laurence Geary paper).

The failure of 1846 resulted in a severe shortage of seed for the 1847 crop. As a result the area planted was only about 25 per cent of that in 1846. In this year the crop flourished and the quantity wassuperb, but because of the shortage of seed planted there was still insufficient food for the population and famine conditions continued. This was the year when mass emigration started and the 'Coffin Ships' prevailed.

1848: The spring of 1848 was very cold and throughout February there were frequent falls of snow. Despite the conditions, there was a revival in the acreage planted following imports of seed from Scotland. However, in mid-July the blight struck again and the crop was destroyed by the end of the month. Emigration continued as the workhouses became over-crowded.

1849: The first few months of 1849 saw as much, if not more, suffering than any of the previous Famine years. However, while the blight was now endemic, the disease caused little loss during the year and the Famine was officially at an end. This coincided with an official visit of Queen Victoria who landed in Cork on 1st August, 1849.

The potato after the Famine

Following the Famine, the potato rapidly regained some of its former popularity and the acreage quickly rose to a peak of about 1.2 million acres in 1859. Apart from a slight increase in the area under potatoes during the First World War the acreage has steadily fallen up to the present day. This fall in acreage was accompanied by an increase in the standards of living and a dramatic reduction in per capita potato consumption. There were a number of failures of the crop after the Famine which were all caused by late blight. These did not cause similar suffering as the dependence on the potato had reduced and the government's relief services were quickly and effectively put into action.

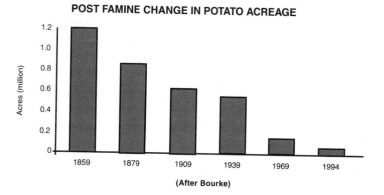

POST FAMINE CHANGE IN POTATO ACREAGE

(After Bourke)

Husbandry after the Famine also changed significantly with the plough largely replacing hand cultivation and the introduction of new varieties, such as Champion, with some resistance to late blight. The Landlord and Tenant Acts also improved the system of land tenure. While in 1885, Millardet was carrying out his first field experiments on the efficacy of the 'Bordeaux Mixture' which was ultimately to lead to the 'cure' for potato late blight.

The causal agent

After the initial outbreak of the disease (potato late blight) there was a major search to establish the underlying cause. As might be expected, this led to a certain level of scientific controversy, in that one group maintained that it was due to natural causes such as the weather, while the other group took the unpopular view that it was caused by a fungus.

Among those who supported the fungal theory were J. E. Teschemacher (USA), van den Hecke, Prof. Charles Morren, Charles Montagne and the Rev. Myles Berkeley. Later Moore was also convinced. Charles Montagne first described the fungus to a meeting of the *Societe Philomatique* in Paris on August 30th, 1845 and named it *Botrytis infestans*. Later, the Rev. Myles Berkeley lent his considerable weight to the fungal theory but it was not until the 1860s that de Bary finally unveiled the full life cycle of the fungus. The science of plant pathology was born and the fungus got its final title of *Phytophthora infestans* (Mont.) de Bary.

The fungus *Phytophthora infestans* (Mont.) de Bary is an Oomycete (Class) which belongs to the family Pythiaceae. This species is characterised by coenocytic mycelium and the production of biflagellate, motile zoospores. The fungus is hetrothallic and can reproduce sexually in the presence of an opposite mating type.

Sexual reproduction follows fertilisation of an oogonium by an antheridium resulting in the production of an oospore. Overwintering can be in the form of resting mycelium (most usual) or oospores. After germination both will result in the production of

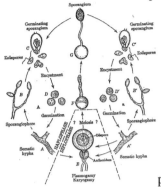

Life cycle of *Phytophthora infestans* as outlined by de Bary in the 1860s.

sporangia which can germinate directly by means of a germ tube or indirectly by means of the motile zoospores. Indirect germination is favoured by short periods of exposure to temperatures below 10°C.

Germination is followed by encystment and appresorium formation. Penetration of the leaf surface is by means of an infection peg followed by intercellular invasion with penetration of the cells by means of an haustorium. Invasion of the leaf is rapid eventually resulting in necrosis and death of the leaf tissue. Under favourable conditions, the sporangiophores emerge through the stomata with a fresh crop of sporangia within 4 to 5 days of the initial infection. This multicycle, air-borne pathogen can therefore spread rapidly within crops and from one crop to another following the initial infection.

The origin and spread of the disease

For many years after the life cycle of *Phytophthora infestans* had been confirmed by de Bary in the 1860s there was a major search to find the perfect stage of the fungus. The lack of success which accompanied this task was surprising in that the perfect stage seemed to be common in related species and genera. Clinton[15] in 1911 presented the first authentic report of oospores in pure culture. Nearly 50 years later the perfect stage was confirmed as occurring naturally in Mexico.[16]

In 1993 Neiderhauser[17] put forward the argument that because the two different mating types were only found in Mexico, where they occurred in a 1:1 ratio, that Mexico was the centre of origin of the fungus. He supports this argument with the fact that vertical and horizontal sources of resistance to the fungus such as *Solanum demissum* are also found in their wild state in Mexico. How the pathogen escaped from Mexico in the first instance is unknown, but Neiderhauser suggests that only one mating type (A1) was involved in this initial escape.

How the pathogen first got to Europe seems to be more clear. Prior to 1845, Bourke and Lamb have shown that *Phytophthora infestans* was recorded in the north-eastern area of the USA between 1843 and 1845. For some years prior to that, a disease known as 'taint' or *Fusarium* dry rot was prevalent in Europe and trials with resistant cultivars from different countries were carried out in Europe. Large scale imports of the more promising varieties seem to have been brought into Belgium from the USA for the 1844 planting season. At harvest time some discoloration and rotting took place in storage.[18]

The disease would appear to have come in on these imports as the disease was present in Belgium by the end of June 1845. According to Bourke and Lamb, it spread from there to the low countries by mid-July, to other parts of Europe and southern England by mid-August and later to Ireland where it is reported that the first observation of its occurrence was by Moore on 20th August, 1845 in the Dublin area.[19]

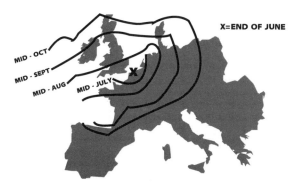

Spread of potato blight in Europe in 1845.

The cure

Soon after the first appearance of the disease the search began for a cure. Bourke reports that as early as 1846 a solution of bluestone (copper sulphate) was suggested as a dip treatment for seed potatoes as this had previously been used as a treatment for bunt in cereals. This chemical in conjunction with lime, salt and water was also suggested as a soil disinfectant. In 1846, David Moore who was curator of the Botanic Gardens in Dublin experimented with a copper sulphate seed dip. This experiment was unsuccessful although it was thought at the time to delay the onset of the disease. Bourke also notes that there were reports that (copper) fumes from a factory in Wales prevented the disease in the vicinity of the factory. Dusting with flowers of sulphur was also suggested as this had been used against *Erysiphe*.

Despite the fact that they were so close to the cure in the 1840s, it was not until forty years later that the remedy was eventually found. This was as a result of Millardet's chance observation in 1882 that grapes in a French vineyard bordering a road which had been sprayed with a mixture of copper sulphate and hydrated lime in order to prevent theft, had remained free from attacks of downy mildew. In 1885 Millardet went on to demonstrate the effectiveness of this treatment in field experiments. The spraying of potatoes did not become universally accepted in Ireland until the beginning of the next century. Bluestone and washing soda remained the universal fungicide for the control of late blight for more than half a century.

In 1934 the first 'organic' fungicides were announced when Du Pont discovered the dithiocarbamates. In the next decade products such as thiram, zineb and maneb became available. Other products such as mancozeb soon followed. Because of their ease of application and the high price of copper on world markets, these gradually replaced the Burgundy mixture and the protectant fungicide mancozeb is still the main ingredient in most control programmes today.

The next important step in the control of late blight was the discovery of the phenylamides in the mid 1970s. They were extremely effective and were used almost exclusively for a number of years until resistance became a problem. They are now only used in conjunction with mancozeb in an anti-resistance strategy. About the same time you had the introduction of the first translaminar product in the form of cymoxanil.

The 1990s have seen the introduction of a number of new products such as fluazinam, dimethomorph and propamocarb. ▒

References

1. R.N. Salaman, (1949). *The history and social influence of the potato.* Cambridge University Press, Cambridge. 685 pages
2. M. S. Hughes, (1991). Potayto, potahto - either way you say it, they a peel *Smithsonian* 22:138-148.
3. W. D. Davidson, (1937). The history of the potato and its progress in Ireland. *Journal of the Department of Agriculture, Republic of Ireland* 34:286-307
4. P. M. A. Bourke, (1993). 'The visitation of God?'. The potato and the great *Irish famine.* Lilliput Press, Dublin. 230 pages.
5. M. S. Hughes, (1991). Potayto, potahto.
6. W. D. Davidson, (1937). The history of the potato and its progress in Ireland.
7. Salaman, (1949). *The history and social influence of the potato.*
8. Davidson, (1937). The history of the potato and its progress in Ireland. *Journal of the Department.of Agriculture, Republic of Ireland* 34:286-307
9. Davidson, (1937). The history of the potato and its progress in Ireland.
10. Salaman, (1949). *The history and social influence of the potato.*
11. Bourke, (1993). 'The visitation of God?'. Lilliput Press, Dublin.
12. Salaman, (1949). *The history and social influence of the potato.*
13. Salaman, (1949). *The history and social influence of the potato.*
14. Charles Nelson, (1983). David Moore, Miles J. Berkeley and scientific studies of potato blight in Ireland, 1845-1847. *Archives of Natural History* 11:249-261
15. G.P. Clinton, (1911). Oospores of potato blight. *Science* 33:744-747
16. M.E. Gallegly, and J. Gallindo, (1958). The oospores of Phytophthora infestans in nature in Mexico. *Phytopathology* 48:274-277.
17. J.S. Neiderhauser, (1993). International cooperation in potato research and development. *Annual Review of Phytopathohogy* 31:1-21
18. P.M.A. Bourke, and H. Lamb. (1993). *The spread of potato blight in Europe in 1845-6 and the accompanying weather patterns.* Meteorological Service, Dublin.
19. Nelson, (1983). David Moore, Miles J. Berkeley and scientific studies of potato blight in Ireland, 1845-1847. *Archives of Natural History* 11:249-261

FOOD SUPPLY AND FOOD RIOTS

Andrés Eiríksson

The historiography of the Great Irish Famine has surprisingly little to say about food riots and other forms of social unrest in connection with the crisis. Until recently the prevailing view was that the popular response to the calamity was an almost immediate resignation and prostration, with acts of defiance being scarce, ineffective and of a personal rather than collective nature. This view is expressed by Cecil Woodham-Smith in *The Great Hunger,* claiming that "Protests ... were few and violence rare; the general feeling was despair. Fear of famine was in the Irish people's blood; only too clearly they realised that they were helpless before the fate overtaking them and turned blindly to those in authority for salvation."[1] This, however, is hard to reconcile with the pre-Famine tradition of popular protest and rural violence in many parts of the country.

In the last few decades before the Famine, roughly from 1815 to 1845, the people of rural Ireland were renowned for their unruly nature, contempt for authority and indeed their frequent acts of violent social protest. Given this tradition, one could expect some sort of active and violent popular resistance with the onset of the Famine. And, as I hope to demonstrate, this was indeed the case.[2]

The main reason why this aspect of the Famine has been largely overlooked is that historians have mostly concentrated on the administrative, economic and demographic facets of the Famine, using official publications as their main source of information. It is to be hoped that increasing emphasis on regional and micro-studies and the use of sources such as police reports, local newspapers, estate papers and folklore material will, amongst other things, shed some light on the popular reaction to the Famine and the way in which it affected personal and social relations.

Social protest

The breakdown of prevailing social relations during the Famine was reflected in a dramatic increase in the number of criminal offences. As Table 1 shows, the number of recorded crimes in 1847 was 20,986, compared to 6,327 in 1844. The crime rate began to fall again in the latter part of 1847, but remained high throughout the Famine and did not fall to pre-Famine levels until the early 1850s. Of course, crime and social protest are far from being synonymous, even if in the mid-nineteenth century the link between the two was much closer than it is now. By far the most common crime during the Famine, and the one which increased the most, was theft. Generally, theft during the Famine was an act of desperation committed by people acting on their own rather than as collectives, with the aim of alleviating immediate want rather than affecting class relations and social policy in the long run. It was an act strongly related to the daily struggle for survival, but it was hardly an act of social protest or one reflecting a particular political stand.

There was, however, one type of theft or plundering which during the Famine was listed as a separate category in crime statistics to distinguish it from other types of thefts, for the very reason that it had a wider social dimension. This was the offence of "plundering provisions". Generally, acts thus labelled were committed by groups of people, often large groups of hundreds or even thousands. They attacked mills, shops, corn stores, soup kitchens, boats and carts transporting corn and meal, and sometimes turnip and cabbage fields of farmers and landlords. Many of these acts were more akin to food riots than thefts, in that their main aim was not to steal food, but rather to regulate the price and the distribution of food.

Many other offences committed at the time were indicative of social conflict. Most of these were listed in crime statistics as "offences against the public peace": crimes such as administering unlawful oaths; stealing or demanding fire arms; riots; illegal meetings; digging up land, etc. I have grouped together all "plundering of provisions" and "offences against the public peace", other than threatening notices and letters, and labelled them as "protest crimes". The total number of these offences indicates the relative level of social unrest each year. This is not to say that every act of this kind was in connection with social protest or that social protest could not be expressed through other criminal acts. But the relationship between social protest and protest crimes as here defined was stronger than in the case of offences listed as personal violence, crimes against property and threatening letters.

Most types of "protest crimes" increased during the Famine and peaked in 1846 and 1847, indicating a high level of social unrest and popular protest, particularly in late 1846 and early 1847. The rise in protest crime and crime in general in 1846 may have been even more dramatic than the official figure allows. The sudden rise in crime in 1846 took the authorities by surprise and in most cases police reinforcements were not sent to the counties until late 1846 or early 1847. Many police duties suffered as a result, including crime detection and reporting. It is likely that relatively large number of crimes went undetected and unrecorded in 1846.

TABLE 1: NUMBER OF RECORDED CRIMES IN IRELAND 1844-52

Type of crime	1844	1845	1846	1847	1848	1849	1850	1851	1852
Physical violence	1,211	1,282	1,472	1,110	1,043	1,189	1,126	1,136	1,238
Destruction of property and animals	750	750	752	1,091	1,009	1,382	1,173	1,014	899
Theft	1,583	1,487	4,791	13,388	9,104	9,949	6,184	5,041	3,522
"Protest crime"	1,494	2,315	3,250	4,130	1,886	1,493	1,016	875	1,030
Illegal letters and notices	862	1,944	1,783	951	784	645	821	686	776
Other crimes	472	319	333	316	254	304	319	392	329
TOTAL	6,327	8,088	12,380	20,986	14,080	14,908	10,639	9,144	7,824

Sources: Chief Secretary's Office: Constabulary Office: Monthly Printed Outrages, 1844 - 1845;
Irish Crime Records 1848 - 1878 (National Archives, Dublin).

It is important not to confuse popular protest with so called "agrarian outrages". In 1844 the constabulary began to list separately crimes of an agrarian nature, believed to be caused by the struggle between tenants and landlords, concerning such issues as rent, evictions, the distribution of farms and so on, and very often constituting attacks on landlords, agents, bailiffs and other people acting on behalf of landlords. These "agrarian outrages" actually decreased during this period of an otherwise high crime rate and intense social unrest. Their number was recorded as 1,920 in 1845, decreasing to 1,303 in 1846 and to a very low 620 in 1847.[3] This suggests that the wave of unrest that swept many parts of Ireland in 1846- 47 had very little to do with evictions or rack rent or other issues in connection with the long - standing struggle for land and the conflict between tenant and landlord. Instead, the unrest was directly related to Famine relief and government policy, concerning the issues of work , wages and the price and distribution of food.

This unrest affected some parts of the country more than others. Judging from the number of protest crimes per thousand of population in each area it appears that there was a particularly disturbed area consisting of north Munster, part of the midlands and east Connacht. This area included Counties Clare, Limerick, Tipperary, Offaly, Westmeath, Longford, Roscommon and Leitrim. It did not include many counties which suffered greatly during the Famine, such as Galway, Mayo, Sligo and Cork.[4] Clearly, it was not the amount of destitution and suffering which alone determined the level of popular protest during the Famine.

More important was the existing tradition of rural unrest and violent protest, particularly in connection with food prices, conacre and other issues concerning the rural poor. Such a tradition existed in most parts of the disturbed area, especially in north Munster, including Clare and Limerick. The remainder of this article is devoted to these two counties, attempting to establish the pattern of food riots and lower class protest in the Clare and Limerick region in the 1830s and 1840s and in particular during the disturbed months of 1846- 47.

It is a long and still widely held view that food riots did not occur or were extremely rare in pre-Famine Ireland.[5] Again, I believe this to be incorrect, reflecting a lack of detailed local studies. Food riots certainly occurred in Clare and Limerick and many other parts of south-west Ireland in 1817, 1822, 1830-31 and especially in the late 1830s and early 1840s, even if that particular period did not witness anything which could be described as famine or fatal scarcity.

Although there were no disastrous years in the decade prior to the Great Famine, there were certainly years of hardship and strife for the labouring population. One indication of this is the rising price of potatoes during this period. On the market in Ennis in Co. Clare the annual average price of potatoes ranged from 3d to 4¼ d per stone in 1837- 42, compared to 2d to 3¾d in 1827-36. In other words, the price of potatoes was over 20 per cent higher in 1837-42 than during the previous ten years. (The market reports do not specify the type of potatoes, but simply give the lowest and the highest price each market day).[6] It appears that the availability, or the supply of potatoes in relation to the mouths to feed, was decreasing. We can quite safely presume that rising prices reflected increasing demand locally rather than higher export prices, as about 98 per cent of Irish potato production was used within Ireland and a large proportion of it was consumed locally.[7]

The price of potatoes was over 20 per cent higher in 1837 - 42
than during the previous ten years.

In this decade prior to the Famine there were a few critical years, 1837, 1839, 1840, 1841 and 1842, when potato prices were high for at least part of the year, reflecting a rather poor harvest the previous year. It was in those years that the summer months, the "hungry weeks" of June and July, became particularly difficult. Labourers and cottiers were liable to run out of potatoes in June or even as early as May, and from then until the new harvest in August they had to rely on potatoes or other food bought from grocers, farmers or landlords. It was in those years, therfore, that potato prices became the concern of the rural poor.

The "rules of the country"

The response of the poor in Limerick and Clare was almost inevitably to establish, through organised physical attacks and threatening notices, a system of intimidation and violence, the purpose of which was to persuade those with potatoes to sell to do so locally and at a price which the poor could afford. It was mainly the better off farmers who bore the brunt of such violence. Their homes were attacked and broken into, they and their families were assaulted and forced to take an oath to the effect that they would not charge more for their potatoes than a certain stipulated price.

For example, on the night of the 21st of March 1837 seven farmers in the parish of Kilkeedy in Co. Limerick were visited by an armed group of upwards of 20 men. This party attacked their houses, broke doors and windows and ordered the farmers to sell their potatoes at 8 or 10 shillings per barrel and to rent out land for conacre.[8] One of the farmers, the Widow Massy of Newtown, had already been attacked two weeks previously by a group of eight men who broke her windows and fired two shots into her house. "Before their departure they told her that she had sent a load of potatoes to market and that their commands should be obeyed".[9] Thomas McGrath of Clonreddan in Co. Clare received similar treatment on the 6th of May 1839, when he was visited by eight or nine armed men with their faces blackened who broke into his home and dragged him outside. He was forced to take an oath to the effect that he would sell his potatoes for no more than £1 per barrel and return money to people he had already charged £2 per barrel.[10]

These nocturnal attacks were usually executed by groups of between 5 and 20 men, often armed and sometimes wearing white shirts or female clothes as a type of Whiteboy uniform. They were often referred to as the Whiteboys, the Rockites or, particularly in Co. Clare, as the Terry Alts or the men of Lady Clare. They originated in the peasant disturbances which swept the county in 1829-31 and were militant representatives of the agricultural labourers and cottiers.[11] Their aim was to put a ceiling on potato prices in times of hardship, to establish what they saw as the "fair price" as opposed to the market price. They were the guardians of what may be called "the moral economy" of the potato trade.[12]

The principles of this moral economy were outlined in illegal notices and letters which accompanied every outbreak of food related violence. Anonymous notices were posted on chapel gates and other public places and sometimes threatening letters were sent to people's homes. These established the price at which potatoes should be sold, distinguishing between different types of potatoes and often between different ways of payment, allowing higher prices if credit was given. They also included threat of death and destruction to anyone who disobeyed these "rules of the country", as in the following letter sent to a farmer in the parish of Kilkeedy in Co. Limerick in April 1837:

> My Dear Friend we have got informations repeatedly that you have charged an exorbitant and unreasonable price for your potatoes I am informed that you charged a poor Widow called Mary O'Brien fifteen shillings per Barrel another poor man who has a large helpless family Named Dickson and several others in the neighbourhood be it known to you my friend that you must go according to the rules of the Country ten shillings for the quality called Cups and Lumpers eight shillings per Barrel I request and insist on your returning the Balance in readiness or if not that you will undergo the punishment of mangling and Laceration in a most brutal manner.[13]

In May 1839 the following notice was posted on the gate of Glanbonan Glebe in Feakle in Co. Clare, referring to exportation of potatoes outside of the locality:

Notice - - -
          All persons are hereby required to take due Notice That any person or persons having the Assurance to charge over 3 pence for White potatoes 3½ pence per cups his coffin will be his Domb if he goes beyond the rules of the Terry alts As for strangers they are Welcome here so as they wont go beyond The Rules of the Country if they Do Their cars will be cut ...
                              Corrofin Boys

Any person that takes this down will be sorry.[14]

One interesting aspect of these campaigns of intimidation and violence is that they were not carried out during the hungry weeks of late June and July, when, for example, theft, begging, vagrancy and other poverty related behaviour peaked. Instead they occurred as early as March and mostly in April, May and early June, before the price of potatoes rose or when it had just started to rise. This shows that these attacks were not simply a "rebellion of the belly", a spontaneous violence of hungry, angry and desperate people. On the contrary, they were carefully planned and calculated operations, based on a good knowledge of potato supply in the locality and an understanding of the market and price movement. They were meant to halt an imminent rise in food prices and to prevent a predictable hardship in the forthcoming weeks and months. To some extent they succeeded, serving to keep down the price of potatoes in the summer months.[15]

There was one major exception to this, namely 1842. That year potato prices remained low for the first five months and no disturbances took place in the spring. But in late May there was a very sudden and rapid rise in prices which appeared to have taken people by some surprise. The result was a wave of food riots in

Ennis, Limerick, Cork and many other towns in the south-west of Ireland in June and July 1842, when large crowds gathered to attack mills, stores, carts and vessels carrying meal and corn, and in some cases managed to force the sale of meal locally at a reduced price.[16] This was the last outbreak of food related disturbances before the Great Famine.

It should now be clear that already, before the Famine, there was in Clare and Limerick a tradition of violence and intimidation in times of dearth: a tradition of lower class organisation, the aim of which was to monitor and regulate the price and distribution of food. It was therefore not surprising that the Famine provoked a strong and violent response by the poor. A wave of food and labour disturbances swept the two counties in late 1846 and early 1847. In Co. Clare I have found records of approximately 120 violent acts in connection with the disturbances from September 1846 to June 1847, involving roughly 20,000 to 30,000 participants. Although most parts of the County were affected to some extent, by far the most disturbed area was the south-east region and the area around Ennis. This included the baronies of Bunratty Lower, Bunratty Upper, Tulla Lower and eastern Islands. It is no coincidence that this area was also the one most disturbed before the Famine and was traditionally the hotbed of the Terry Alts, labour militancy and food related violence.

Judging by crime statistics, Limerick was even more disturbed than Clare, but unfortunately only a small proportion of Co. Limerick police reports have survived. It is therefore difficult to quantify and locate the disturbances in Co. Limerick. However, from the remaining records it appears that in Limerick, as in Clare, the traditionally more disturbed eastern part was the main area of riots and disaffection. The baronies of Shanid, Glenquin and Connello Upper seem to have been relatively quiet. In total, there must have been several hundred acts of collective violence in connection with labour issues and the food trade in Clare and

Limerick committed in late 1846 and early 1847. This was the most extensive wave of peasant disturbances in the area since the Terry Alt rebellion in 1831.

The unrest in 1846 and 1847 differed in many ways from the food related disturbances of former years. For various reasons the Famine changed the pattern and the purpose of food riots and labour unrest. Obviously, the disturbances no longer centred around the potato. Regulating the sale and the price of potatoes became of little relevance as most of the crop disappeared and potatoes were no longer the staple diet of the poor. Instead, attention turned to the trade in corn and meal. Also, the various changes in people's social environment and economic activities induced by the Famine resulted in a new pattern of lower class organisation and collective action.

Famine riots

The Famine riots can be divided into four main categories on the basis of their aims, pattern, targets and timing. Firstly, there were attempts to secure employment and protect wages on the public works. Such actions began in the summer of 1846, became more frequent in September and peaked in October and November. Secondly, there were attacks and riots the purpose of which was to prevent grain from being exported and to lower the price of meal. Such actions began in the autumn of 1846 and continued throughout the devastating period of inflating meal prices from September 1846 to January 1847. Thirdly, there was a determined and violent resistance to the closure of the public works in the spring of 1847. This resistance was partly directed against the soup kitchens, which in the beginning were opposed by a large proportion of the poor. And finally, once the soup kitchens had been accepted, there occurred in May and June 1847 food riots meant to influence the management of the kitchens and secure larger and better rations.

Much of the violence in connection with the public works was directed against senior staff, such as engineers, stewards, inspectors and especially overseers. The latter were in daily contact with the workers, who regularly assaulted and harassed them. This violence served several purposes. Firstly, it may have served to keep up wages, which under the task work system depended to some extent on the assessment of overseers and other senior staff. Secondly, it prevented a too rigorous control by overseers and others over labourers and their work. This was important in times of growing want and hunger, when energy had to be saved and too much hard work avoided. Finally, and perhaps most importantly, the violence was supposed to increase employment and prevent discharges and often occurred in the wake, of or in anticipation of, discharges.

The first attacks of this kind occurred as early as July 1846. A steward and an overseer were attacked and seriously injured near Bruff in Co. Limerick by small groups of workers in protest against reduction of works. Describing these incidents, Thomas Kearny, a public works engineer, complained that :

> the overseers and stewards have lost all control over the workmen, who now do what they like and as they like and scarcely a day occurs that some shameful outrage is not perpetrated on some one, more especially on those who attempt to perform their duty.[17]

Such attacks were common until January 1847. On the 27th of November 1846 an overseer at Belvoir in Co. Clare was attacked by five armed men with their faces blackened and wearing female clothes. They assaulted him "till nearly dead in the presence of 2 gangs of workmen ...". [18]

About a month later an overseer named Harrington in Ruan, Co. Clare, was visited by night, dragged out of bed by a group of ten men, while twenty more waited outside. Afterwards a local engineer complained that "both the overseers & the stewards are quite at the mercy (both day and night) of the workmen". [19]

Usually this violence against public works management was not life threatening. Fire arms were often worn but seldom used. Taken too far the violence might backfire and result in temporary or permanent discharges. This happened, for example, in the case of the near fatal shooting of Martin Hennessy on the 5th of December 1846, a short distance from Clare Castle.[20] None of the many witnesses to the shooting came to Hennessy's assistance and none was willing to assist the police in the subsequent investigation. As a punishment, 900 people were laid off the works for nearly a month. Two weeks after the shooting Captain Wynne, public works inspector, found the people in the area "sullen and sulky". Nothing, he said, "can exceed the distress and the destitution of the people in Clare Abbey". [21]

Attacks on overseers and other public works staff were usually carried out either by an individual acting alone or by small groups of men. But in 1846 there were also other actions in connection with the public works of a more collective nature, being either riots, peaceful demonstrations or even strikes. The first recorded industrial strike in Clare occurred on 20th of August 1846 when "labourers employed upon the road in progress at either side of Gore's-quay, near Ennis, broke off work ... in consequence of the Board of Work giving notice of a reduction of their wages to eight pence per day...". [22] In mid-October public works labourers in various parts of the county went on strike, this time against the introduction of the new task work system, which linked wages to performance.[23] Throughout October and until mid-November demonstrations and serious riots occurred in both counties against task works.

In early November a large crowd of public works labourers gathered in Newcastle in Co. Limerick in protest against task works. They surrounded the courthouse during a session of the relief committee, threatening to attack the courthouse and shouting "no task work" and "no tickets". They verbally and physically attacked an engineer whom they held responsible for the introduction of the new system. Throughout the day "multitudes of turbulent people" were said to be "patrolling the streets, sounding horns at different places ...". [24] At the same time riots and demonstrations occurred in various parts of Co. Clare. A serious riot took place in Clare Castle

were the labourers acted "as the whole country was at their mercy ..."
and about 400 labourers marched through the village of Cooraclare,
demanding the abolition of task works and a fixed rate of 1 shilling
per day.[25] No doubt, a performance-related wage system in the
midst of hunger and want was a bad and cruel idea. Initially, many
labourers experienced it as a means of wage reduction and
discrimination. In the long run, however, it did not affect the
average wages on the works, which until June 1847 ranged from
10d. to 1s.1d. per day. By the latter part of November opposition to
the system had ceased.

Opposition to exportation of grain

But while nominal wages remained at the same level, real wages
dropped rapidly as the price of food inflated after August 1846. In
many places the price of oatmeal and Indian meal, now the staple
diet of the poor, doubled or even trebled from October 1846 to
January 1847. Demonstrations for higher wages occurred
occasionally and attacks on public works staff continued. But
increasingly the poor turned their attention to the corn trade,
attempting to lower the price of food. This was a more traditional
method than wage struggle and one more likely to succeed, as it was
directed mostly against farmers, merchants and other individuals
rather than the government itself.

Attempts to prevent the exportation of corn began in Co. Clare
in the autumn of 1846. A series of Whiteboy attacks were carried
out during the harvest, consisting mainly of the ambushing and
shooting of horses involved in the transportation of corn. This
campaign took place almost exclusively in the fertile area of south-
east Clare, where corn was transported by horses and carts to Ennis
and Limerick. The horses were shot on their way to the towns or on
their return, as a deterrent against further exportation. The
constabulary concluded, probably correctly, that smallholders and
labourers in that area had "formed a combination to intimidate
bysuch acts the rich farmers from disposing of their corn ...". [26]

_1917_

Shannon Navigation
Clare Castle Octr 5th 1846.

Name of Work
or
Subject of Letter } on a popular Tumult

Sir,

I have now to inform the Commissioners of the Board of Public Works, that, this day at 12 o'clock, that a number of distressed laborers from this and the adjoining Parishes to the number of from 400 to 500, proceeded to the wharf at Clare and turned back the horses and Cars laden with Oats for shipment on a Smack & 3 Hookers taking in their Cargoes at the Quay for Limerick, warning the Boatmen not to attempt to take any more of the provision of the County away on the peril of their lives. To describe to the Commissioners the state of this village & the surrounding Parishes is impossible, the destitution has prevailed to an alarming extent. It is not safe to reside within its precincts and had it not been for the vigilance of the Police it would be awfully bad.

I remain Sir
your obedient Servant
M. H. Hennessy

The Secretary Board
of Public Works
Dublin

A letter from Martin Hennessy to the Board of Public Works dated 5th of October 1846. The letter tells of the first action taken by Co. Clare labourers in protest against the exportation of grain.

But this campaign was short lived and limited to a small area. It occurred mostly in September 1846 and all but ceased the following month.

By then a new method had been adopted by the poor. Food riots proper, involving large crowds of dozens, hundreds or even thousands of people had begun and continued with regularity for several months. The first Famine food riot in the area took place on the 5th of October 1846, when about 400 to 500 labourers gathered in Clare Castle and turned back horses and carts laden with oats about to be taken by boats to Limerick City. They warned the boatmen never "to take any more of the provisions of the County away on the perils of their lives ...". [27] Other similar instances followed, prompting numerous requests from landlords, farmers and merchants for police or military escort of corn and meal. By the 20th of October 1846 it was reported that "no vessel will pass up the river Fergus, laden with meal or grain, without an escort".[28]

Opposition to exports was strongest in south-east Clare, around Ennis, north-east Limerick and around Limerick City. On the 28th and 29th of October several thousands people rioted in O'Brien's Bridge and Scarriff in Co. Clare, attacking boats, mills and shops. Millers in the two towns were compelled to lower the price of oatmeal and one of them, Mr. Walnut of Scarriff, was forced to return the balance between the new price and his previous price to some of his customers.[29] Although some pilfering took place, the main aim of the rioters was to prevent exports and to lower prices. This was generally the case in the beginning, but pilfering increased as the Famine continued. This was in contrast with the food disturbances in the 1830s and early 1840s, when pilfering was extremely rare. During the Famine the line between food riots and collective plundering became less clear. Nevertheless, the term "plundering provisions", often used in crime statistics for this sort of activity, is somewhat misleading, as the principal purpose was to negotiate prices through the use or the threat of violence and to prevent grain from being transported to Limerick City and subsequently exported.

The rationale behind the riots was illustrated in the following incident, described by the police as "a triumph to the people ...". On the 31st of October 1846 a large convoy of corn heading for Limerick was met by a crowd of labourers on the Clare and Limerick border, a short distance from O'Brien's Bridge. In spite of military protection it was seized by the crowd and forced to return. There were allegedly 300 to 400 men on the road, mostly public works labourers, "and the fields were crowded with women and children". The crowd declared that they were ready to be shot and "die on the spot", but they would not "suffer the corn to go to Limerick to be sent out of the country, the potatoes were all gone, they had nothing to live on but grain, and while they were starving it was all sending from the country and no food of any kind coming back in return, that they might bring it to O'Briens Bridge and sell it there, but they would oppose it going to Limerick for exportation". [30]

The exportation of grain and other food during the Famine has ever since been a source of much criticism, especially by nationalist commentators. To some extent this criticism may have been misplaced. The government's decision to free the importation of corn rather than restrict exportation appeared to work in 1847 and 1848. During those years high prices in Ireland attracted unprecedented imports of gain. This was true particularly for 1847 when the volume of imports was about six times that of exports. Imports rose from 28,000 tons in 1845 to 889,000 tons in 1847, while at the same time exports dropped from 513,000 tons to 146,000 tons.[31] However, it has often been argued that a temporary ban on grain exports in late 1846 would have been of enormous benefit in halting the inflation of food prices and increasing greatly the value of the public works. This certainly seems to have been the view of the poor inhabitants of Limerick, Clare and many other parts of north Munster, west Leinster and east Connacht. Indeed, they, and they alone, were engaged in an active and organised resistance against the exportation of corn. During this struggle they confronted not only Anglo-Irish landlords and government forces, but to no less extent Irish farmers, millers, shopkeepers and workers involved in the transportation of grain. The conflict between exportation and trade restriction was a conflict not only between Irish and English interests or between peasants and landlords, it was also a conflict within the Irish agricultural community, between the starving poor on the one hand and commercially minded farmers and tradespeople on the other.

Work, not porridge

The opposition to exports came to a halt in late January 1847 once food prices stabilised and began to decrease. At the same time as more and more people were employed on the public works, rioting ceased and the area was relatively quiet in February and March 1847. But in late March disturbances started again, increasing gradually in April and peaking in May and early June. The reason was the abolition of the public works in March to June 1847. In Co. Clare the riots began immediately when the plans for the discharges were made known. The bearer of the news to Newmarket-on-Fergus, Capt. Fishbourne, was surrounded by a large crowd who greeted him with verbal abuses and threats, shouting "Blood is better than starvation". He was hit on the head with a stone and, according to the police, were it not for their own interference he would have been drowned in the river Fergus.[32]

During April, May and June people frequently assembled outside the meetings of local relief committees and the residents of public work inspectors and superintendents, using menacing language and on occasion attacking people and property in an unsuccessful bid to reverse the discharges and the closure of the works. On many occasions discharged labourers attacked and plundered stores and mills, threatening to continue to do so until they were re-employed. On the 7th of May about 200 people attacked the mill at Croagh in Co. Limerick and carried away nineteen bags of flour. The following day the magistrates in that neighbourhood issued a petition to Dublin Castle, lamenting the "alarming state in which the district is at present ... owing to the stoppage of the Public works ...". They described the situation as "armed mobs parading the Country in all directions, plundering provisions in transit, attacking houses by day as well as by night and committing various other depravations to the terror and serious injury of the peaceable and well disposed portion of the community".[33]

Riots such as these occurred during the very disastrous gap in relief measures in April and May, when the public works were rapidly being abolished while the establishment of the soup kitchens were painfully slow. But even when the soup kitchens finally began to operate this did not immediately quell the riots. In fact, particularly in Co. Clare, the opening of the soup kitchens seemed to lead to increased rioting. It is interesting to note, although the public works have been criticised by later historians and the public alike, as a rather cruel and ineffective means of relief, that at the time of the Famine the poor themselves in many parts of the country much preferred the works to other forms of relief and made their opinion known in no uncertain manner.[34] On the 10th of May 1847 a crowd of several hundred people attacked the newly established

soup kitchen at Meelick in Co. Clare, destroyed the boiler and all other utensils and tore up the book of the relief committee. They also destroyed the boiler at Cloonlara and tried to do the same in Ardnacrusha, but were prevented by the police.

In the course of these disturbances the crowd gathered outside the house of a local J.P. and informed him that they wanted employment and "would not put up with and endure the use of soup or porridge ...". [35] This attitude was frequently expressed during the 1847 food and labour riots in Clare. On the 14th of May the soup kitchen in Kilfenora was attacked by a crowd who carried away the boiler.[36] The *Limerick Reporter* explained that the people loudly called for work and "abhor the idea of being made beggars".[37] Thus, the main objection of the poor to the soup kitchens was that this system of relief reduced them to the status of pauper.

There was in pre-Famine rural Ireland a definite stigma attached to pauperism and begging and this was still the case in 1847. On the public works the former farm labourers and cottiers still earned their living by labour, if not always a particularly useful labour. For these people the soup kitchens symbolised a drop in social status: they had now become beggars. The opposition to the soup kitchens was also based on people's profound dislike of the soup, or the porridge as it was often called. They made it clear that they would much rather receive either money or uncooked meal. Of course, receiving wages instead of cooked food had one advantage, namely that wages could be used to pay for emigration. The possibility of this option was reduced by the closure of the public works.

However, the resistance to the soup kitchens was only temporary. The poor soon accepted the fact that the public works were not going to re-open and that government policy in this regard was not likely to change. From mid-May to mid-June the resistance to the soup kitchens was gradually replaced by attempts by the poor to influence the management of the kitchens, the size of rations, the number of stations and the type of food that was served. On the

15th of June the town of Kilrush in Clare was in a state of disturbance "in consequence of the unwillingness of those receiving relief to take cooked food as they preferred receiving their rations in meal, and cooking it themselves." A large crowd of people surrounded the William's Hotel where Poor Law Inspector Capt. Hill resided, they attacked the hotel with stones and broke several windows. The riot ended when Capt. Hill appeared before the crowd and promised to give out meal instead of soup until the next meeting of the relief committee.[38]

On several occasions riots of this kind brought some, albeit temporary, success. In mid-May about 500 people gathered around the courthouse in Ennistymon and demanded more relief stations and uncooked meal instead of soup. They attacked the house and attempted to demolish the boiler, but were resisted by a strong constabulary party and forced to withdraw. Immediately afterwards a meeting of the poor law guardians agreed to open a new station in the parish of Clooney and to substitute soup with meal. However, the soup was re-introduced in Ennistymon ten days later, which caused a great uproar in the town. Riots were anticipated and troops sent in to assist the police. Presumably because of the presence of the military, no rioting took place but protest marches and peaceful demonstrations were staged.[39]

It is very clear from this and other similar events that people disliked the soup and much preferred meal, which they could cook themselves. From the government's point of view, serving cooked food instead of meal prevented inadequate cooking facilities and lack of hygiene in people's homes from aggravating already widespread diarrhoea and dysentery. Also, it was claimed that serving meal led to corrupting practices such as trading meal for tea, tobacco and alcohol. If that was the case, it may explain some of the resistance against the soup. But,more importantly, people still found the soup kitchen degrading and preferred to receive meal which they could cook and eat in the privacy of their own home. They also simply disliked the soup which they often found very watery and disagreeable.

The food riots in connection with the soup kitchens in May and June 1847 constituted the last serious Famine disturbances in the area. Once the poor law unions and the workhouses took over the administration of relief in the summer of 1847 Famine riots came to an end. Some riots occurred inside and outside the workhouses from late 1847 onwards, but these were few and far between and, unlike many of the previous riots, invariably ineffective. What was it that caused the cessation of protest in mid-1847? And what was it that caused the initial surge in popular protest and its changing nature in late 1846 and early 1847?

Labour militancy and social unrest

The most obvious explanation for the disturbances in 1846-47 was the Famine itself, the very fact that people were starving or facing starvation, especially since the population in Clare and Limerick already had a tradition of violent resistance in similar if less dramatic circumstances. But the volume and particularly the pattern of the disturbances were also very much the result of the immense changes in people's social status and working environment brought about by the Famine and by various government relief measures. Here, the public works were of paramount importance. Firstly, as we have seen, the public works became a target of protesters, who sought to influence employment, wages and working conditions. Secondly, and more importantly, the public works served as a platform for organisation.

The 1846 mass protests against the exportation of grain were almost always planned and plotted by labourers on the public works, who discussed their tactics during working hours and took time off working for the purpose of rioting. Police reports and petitions of magistrates again and again emphasised this fact, and their comments on this were usually underlined or marked in some way for special attention by the Chief Secretary's Office in Dublin Castle. Those who fought against the closure of the public works in 1847 were also labourers on the works or people who had very recently been discharged. Even many of those who rioted against the soup kitchens in May and June 1847 were recently discharged public works labourers.

Middle and upper class people in Clare and Limerick were very much of the opinion that the public works had the undesirable effect of increasing labour militancy and social unrest. In November 1846 public works inspector Sir Gaspard Le Marchant wrote from Tulla in Co. Clare:

> I have found it to be the opinion of intelligent people in this neighbourhood, that the Public Works, and their system of bringing together large bodies of men, who mutually inflame each other, and plot mischief to remedy the distress of themselves and families, become daily pregnant with the greatest danger to the country. These men, by being brought together in masses, are taught to understand their own strength. [40]

These people, who until recently had been farm labourers and cottiers working in small units and scattered between different farms and villages, now became semi-industrial labourers, working together in large groups under one employer. This increased their potential to organise and protest and resulted in different tactics, as the large rioting crowd replaced the traditional small clandestine Whiteboy group as the main unit of organisation. The novel attempts of Clare public works labourers to organise strikes in 1846 exemplify the way in which popular protest at this early stage of the Famine was becoming increasingly modern and industrialised.

In the same way as the creation of the works stimulated organisation and labour protest, their disappearance discouraged popular protest in the long run. The closure of the works led to an immediate wave of riots and violence, but active resistance soon ceased once the works had been abolished for good and the burden of relief put on the poor law unions. The change from the public works to the workhouses meant that workers became paupers. And while workers are potential protesters and rebels, paupers and beggars are not.

Famine riot in Dungarvan, October 1846.

While increasing hunger, disease and fatigue also played their part, this change in people's social status was probably the main reason for the cessation of popular protest in the latter stages of the Great Famine. By then the poor had become economically inactive. For them, popular protest had become pointless because it no longer had any targets. There was no point in fighting for wages or employment, as there were no potential employers and people were not receiving wages.

Fighting for conacre was also of no use, as the conacre system had crumbled with the disappearance of the potato. For cottiers and smallholders the struggle for land also became pointless, as small plots of land no longer guaranteed survival. To a small extent agrarian crimes against evictions and rent collection continued throughout the Famine, but these were mostly the deeds of larger farmers. The near landless labourers, cottiers and smallholders who bore the brunt of the wholesale Famine evictions in 1848 and onwards put up almost no resistance. In Clare, the infamous Kilrush evictions met with no resistance and in many cases people had already left their plots and houses before they were formally evicted. In other words, by late 1847 popular protest was no longer a sensible tactic in the struggle for survival. This was the main reason for the collapse of popular resistance during the latter part of the Famine, and certainly not any intrinsic fatalism or blind respect for authority.

Far from throwing the Irish poor into immediate despair and submission, the Famine initially, and for almost ten eventful months, prompted a huge wave of often effective and increasingly collective popular protest. ▣

References

1. Cecil Woodham-Smith: *The Great Hunger* (London 1962), pp. 111-2. See also: K. B. Nowlan: "The Political Background" in R. D. Edwards, and T. D. Williams, (eds): *The Great Hunger: Studies in Irish History*, 1845-52 (Dublin 1956), p. 138.
2. Most recent books on the Famine acknowledge the existence of food riots, disturbances and a high level of violence during the Famine. Nevertheless, their extent and importance has not yet been established and is probably under-estimated. See: Daly: *The Famine in Ireland* (Dundalk 1986), p. 86; Peter Gray: *The Irish Famine* (London 1995), pp. 50-1; Christine Kinealy: *This Great Calamity: The Irish Famine* 1845-52 (Dublin 1994), pp. 69, 94, 144-5, 202; Cormac Ó Gráda: *The Great Irish Famine* (Dublin 1989), pp. 43-4.
3. *Irish Crime Records* 1848-1878 (National Archives, Dublin).
4. However, even counties such as Cork and Waterford, which appear to have been relatively undisturbed, witnessed food riots at the early stages of the Famine and these have been the subject of local studies. See: J. S Donnelly: *The Land and the People of Nineteenth Century Cork* (London 1975), pp. 87-91; William Fraher: 'The Dungarvan Disturbances of 1846 and Sequels' in Cowman, Des & Brady, Donald (Eds): *The Famine in Waterford* (Dublin 1995), pp. 137-52.
5. Samuel Clark: *Social Origins of the Irish Land War* (New Jersey 1979), p. 67; Samuel Clark & J. S. Donnelly: *Irish Peasants: Violence and Political Unrest* 1780-1914 (Dublin 1983), pp. 27-28; J. J. Lee: "The Ribbonmen" in Williams, T. D. (ed): *Secret Societies in Ireland* (Dublin 1973), pp. 33-4; J. J Lee: "Patterns of Rural Unrest in Nineteenth Century Ireland: a Preliminary Survey) in L. M. Cullen & F. Furet,(eds): *Ireland and France, 17th-20th Centuries* (Paris 1980), p. 226; G. C. Lewis: *Local Disturbances in Ireland* (1836. Revised edition: Cork 1977), p. 73.
6. The prices were published every week in the *Clare Journal*.
7. P. M. A. Bourke: 'The Use of the Potato Crop Pre-Famine', *Journal of the Statistical and Social Inquiry Society in Ireland*, XII (6), 1968, pp. 72-96.
8. Chief Secretary's Office: Outrage Reports: 17/1837/88. (National Archives, Dublin).
9. Ibid: 17/1837/42.
10. Ibid: 5/1839/3306.
11. On the Terry Alts, see: Andrés Eiríksson: 'Crime and Popular Protest in County Clare, 1815-1852' (PhD. Thesis, TCD, 1991); F. P Enright: 'The Terry Alts' (M.A. Thesis, UCD, 1980).
12. See: Eiríksson (1991), pp. 168-73, 194-206, 363-6.
13. C.S.O.O.R.: 17/1837/136,148.
14. Ibid: 5/1839/3391.
15. Eiríksson (1991), pp. 194-206.
16. Ibid, pp. 202-6.
17. C.S.O.O.R.: 17/1846/21787.
18. Ibid: 5/1846/31163.

19. Ibid: 5/1847/11.
20. Ibid:5/1846/31187,34293,34785,35127,35363,36741,38087;5/1847/25, 38; *Clare Journal,* 10 Dec. 1846; *Limerick Reporter,* 8 Dec. 1846, 11 Dec. 1846; *Tipperary Constitution,* 12 Dec. 1846, 16 Dec. 1846; House of Commons Papers 1847 (764), l, 1: 'Relief of the Distress in Ireland: Correspondence from July 1846 to January 1847 (Board of Work Series)', pp. 309, 311, 313, 341-2, 401.
21. House of Commons Papers 1847 (764), l, 1, p. 424.
22. *Limerick Reporter,* 21 August 1846.
23. Ibid, 16 Oct. 1846; *Clare Journal,* 15 Oct 1846; *Tipperary Constitution,* 21 Oct. 1846; House of Commons Papers 1847 (761), li, 1: 'Relief of the Distressed in Ireland: Correspondence from January 1846 to January 1847 (Commissariat Series)', p. 238.
24. C.S.O.O.R.: 17/1846/30671,31111.
25. *Clare Journal,* 5 Nov. 1846; House of Commons Papers 1847 (764), l,1, p. 309.
26. C.S.O.O.P.: 5/1846/25631.
27. Ibid: 5/1846/27855.
28. House of Commons Papers 1847 (761), li, 1, p. 197.
29. C.S.O.O.R.: 5/1846/29929,29931,29933,29941,30567.
30. Ibid: 17/1846/29875.
31. P. M. A. Bourke: 'The Irish Grain Trade, 1839-48' *Irish Historical Studies,* XX (78), 1976, pp. 156-69.
32. C.S.O.O.R.: 5/1847/251; *Clare Journal,* 25 March 1847, 27 March 1847; *Tipperary Constitution,* 27 March 1847.
33. C.S.O.O.R.: 17/1847/573,592.
34. Kinealy (1995), pp. 145-6.
35. *Limerick Reporter,* 11 May 1847.
36. *Limerick Reporter,* 18 May 1847; *Tipperary Constitution,* 22 May 1847.
37. *Limerick Reporter,* 18 May 1847.
38. Ibid, 18 June 1847; *Clare Journal,* 17 June 1847; *Tipperary Constitution,* 23 June 1847.
39. C.S.O.O.R.: 5/1847/525,526,613; *Clare Journal,* 27 May 1847; *Galway Vindicator,* 2 June 1847; *Limerick Reporter,* 18 May 1847; *Tipperary Constitution,* 19 May 1847, 2 June 1847.
40. House of Commons Papers 1847 (764), l, 1, p. 190.

WHAT PEOPLE DIED OF DURING THE FAMINE

Laurence M. Geary

"Famine and fever and dysentery and diarrhoea are carrying off the population".[1]

The criteria of famine are extreme and protracted shortage of food, resulting in widespread and persistent hunger, emaciation of the affected population and dramatically increased mortality. Ireland's Great Famine presented all of these features in a very pronounced form. Death on an unprecedented scale followed on the repeated failures of the potato crop, the staple food of more than one-third of the country's swollen population. At least 1,000,000 Irish lives were sacrificed to dearth and disease in the mid- and late-1840s. The vast majority succumbed to epidemic infection, some to dietary deficiency diseases, the remainder to starvation.

Starvation

The physical effects of undernutrition include loss of body fat, wasting of skeletal muscle and atrophy of the visceral organs except for the brain and nervous tissue. Sufferers complain of weakness and muscle pains and sit or lie down whenever possible. Movement becomes sluggish and a slow, shuffling gait develops. Nocturnal sleep is interrupted, although total sleep increases gradually. The skin becomes extremely sensitive and bruises easily. Tolerance to noise and cold decreases. Blood pressure and heart rate decline. Oedema (retention of fluid) often occurs, first in the face, then in the extremities, later in the abdominal and thoracic cavities.

There is little impairment of the intellect but the emotions are greatly affected. Victims' moods alternate between apathy and extreme irritability. They become ill-tempered and are easily discouraged and depressed. Concentration and memory lapses become more frequent and speech slows down. Interest in sex diminishes and sexual performance is affected.

Women experience problems with menstruation and spermatogenesis declines in men. Light hair appears on women's faces, while men's beards stop growing. Both sexes lose hair from the top of the head and around the genitals. There is an increasing lack of concern with personal appearance and behavioural constraints are loosened. Body weight falls, basal metabolic rate decreases and activity is reduced to a minimum. Once a 30 per cent weight loss is incurred, the chances of survival are virtually nil without medical intervention. A 40 per cent wastage during famine is almost certainly fatal.

The social impact of famine is equally profound and exacting. There are three clearly identifiable phases in the communal response to such a disaster. The first, which is known as the alarm phase, is triggered by the onset of famine and prompts a co-operative reaction at community level, one marked by the sharing of food and other resources among friends and neighbours. This is a period of intense activity, one characterised by population movements as individuals and families roam in search of food. Markets are often chaotic and food prices soar. Political and religious activity intensifies. There is an increase in the number of spontaneous and concerted outbreaks of violence, often occurring where food and other commodities are in storage or transit.

As the physiological effects of famine become more pronounced and individuals weaken from hunger, a protracted phase of resistance sets in, one in which individual and communal generosity disappear. Conservation of energy becomes paramount and all unnecessary activity ceases. Ritual observances are put off. Religious attendance declines. Lawlessness and physical violence continue to increase but tend to be less concerted and sustained. People congregate only where there is a possibility of obtaining sustenance. Food preparation and consumption take place in secret and supplies are hidden. The search for alternative sources of food intensifies and becomes increasingly desperate.

Eventually, resistance gives way to exhaustion. This is the final phase of famine and is characterised by the gradual unbinding of family ties. Within the household, food sharing becomes increasingly discriminatory. The elderly are seen as a drain on provisions. Tolerance towards children does not erode as quickly, although a time invariably arrives when they too receive disproportionately small amounts of food. Infanticide, suicide and homicide increase at this stage and provide further evidence of the disintegration of the social fabric.[2]

First hand accounts of the Great Famine, particularly by doctors, provide us with a specifically Irish focus on the foregoing characteristics of famine. Dr. Daniel Donovan, who practised in Skibbereen, Co. Cork, was given ample opportunity to study the sensations experienced by the starving. He was told that the pain of hunger was very acute at first but subsided after twenty-four hours and was followed by what his informants described as "a feeling of weakness and sinking", accompanied by a sensation of coldness over the entire surface of the body and an insatiable thirst for cold water. As physical wasting advanced, the eyes took on "a most peculiar stare", the skin exhaled an offensive odour and was covered with a brownish, filthy looking coating, which was almost as

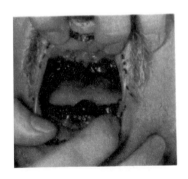 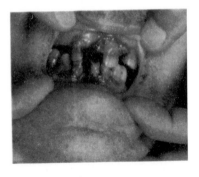

Scurvy, the most common deficiency disease during the Famine

indelible as varnish, according to Donovan. The victim staggered as if drunk, spoke weakly like one suffering from cholera, whined childishly, and burst into tears for no apparent reason. The physical deterioration was accompanied by profound psychological changes. While Donovan did not encounter a single instance of "delirium" or "mania" as a result of prolonged fasting, many were reduced to what he termed "a state of imbecility", others to "almost complete idiotism".

He cited the manslaughter of two local youths, whose throats were cut for the small quantity of Indian meal they possessed, as an instance of starvation induced "mental imbecility". The fourteen year old perpetrator did not consider himself guilty of any crime, nor did he think that he deserved to be or would be punished for his sanguinary deed.

It was Donovan's experience that prolonged food deprivation affected children and adults differently. Starvation appeared to paralyse the will of the adult but sharpened the child's instinct for survival, he noted. As the famine crisis deepened, young and old became increasingly insensitive to the wants and suffering of others, their actions and responses dictated by the desperation of their own needs. Donovan saw mothers snatch food from their starving children, sons and fathers fight over a potato, and parents look on the dead and decaying bodies of their offspring without evincing the slightest emotion.[3]

Several of Donovan's colleagues provided corroborative and equally graphic accounts of the effects of starvation. The very experienced Dr. John Jacob, physician to the Queen's County infirmary at Maryborough, noted the steady physical deterioration, from perfect health to emaciation and debility. Individuals seemed to burn more easily in the sun and the hands, feet, face, and other exposed parts of the body became covered in blisters and ulcers. Bowel complaints degenerated into uncontrollable and often fatal bouts of dysentery. Oedema caused great physical weakness and invariably ended in what Jacob termed "the release of death". Physically shrunken individuals staggered about, their wasted muscles unable to support them. An incalculable number of survivors of famine and starvation-related diseases were left permanently infirm, mutilated and scarred, he said, while death occurred on an almost incomprehensible scale.

"In another world only will stand recorded the number of lives that were lost", he concluded despairingly.[4] Dr. Lynch of Loughrea, Co. Galway, noted the striking pallor and emaciation, the "altered, whispering, whining voice", the distressing feeling of inward sinking. The starving wasted to living skeletons, Lynch continued. They knew they were dying and were resigned to their fate. They lost the will to live and succumbed gently, unprotestingly. In Lynch's words, they seemed "to die by inches".[5]

An uncannily similar image was employed a century later to describe the plight of the 500,000 Polish Jews who were subjected to a regime of mass starvation in the Warsaw ghetto in the early months of 1942. One of their number is reported to have said that their strength was "vanishing like a melting wax candle". According to the physicians who monitored the biological and psychological response of their co-religionists, persistent hunger changed active, busy, energetic people into depressed, apathetic, sleepy beings, always in bed, hardly able to get up to eat or go to the toilet.

Passage from life to death was slow and gradual, like death from physiological old age. There was nothing violent, they recorded, no pain, no obvious change in breathing or circulation. Vital functions subsided simultaneously. Pulse and respiratory rate slowed and it became more and more difficult to reach the patient's awareness, until life was extinguished. People fell asleep in bed or on the street and

Pellegra, a disease triggered by inadequacy of niacin, is characterised by dermatosis, diarrhoea and dementia.

were found dead in the morning. Many died during physical effort, such as searching for food, and sometimes even with a piece of bread in their hands.[6] During the Great Famine, Dr. John Popham of Cork reported that starving individuals used to creep about the streets while their strength allowed, before sinking exhausted in some shed or doorway, where they were often found dead.[7]

Dietary deficiency diseases

A number of vitamin deficiency diseases were detected during the Great Famine, among them xerophthalmia, an eye disease caused by a lack of vitamin A in the diet. Another was pellagra, which is triggered by an inadequacy of Niacin and which is characterised by dermatosis, diarrhoea and dementia. The most common deficiency disease appears to have been scurvy, a potentially fatal ailment caused by an insufficiency of ascorbic acid or vitamin C. Potatoes were the main source of vitamin C for the Irish poor and scurvy appeared rapidly and extensively after the failure of the crop. The initial symptoms of the disease are weakness, breathlessness, exhaustion and mental depression. Later, the gums are livid, spongy, ulcerating and bleeding. Teeth loosen and drop out and the breath is excessively foetid. Bleeding under the surface of the skin causes purple blotches which generally appear first on the limbs and then on other parts of the body. Bleeding into the joints and muscles cause them to swell and become painful.

The further progress of the malady is marked by profound exhaustion, with a tendency to fainting, and with various complications, such as diarrhoea and lung or kidney troubles, any of which may prove fatal.[8] It is not known how may people died of scurvy during the Great Famine. Given the prevalence of the disease, the return of 167 deaths for the decade ending 1851, recorded in the census of that year, is risible, a fact acknowledged by William Wilde, the census commissioner responsible for compiling the medical statistics.

Infectious disease

During famine, two factors, often working in tandem, facilitate the occurrence of epidemics. These are the impairment of the individual immune system by starvation and the loss of community resistance to the spread of disease.[9] Ireland's three long-standing epidemic scourges, "fever", dysentery and smallpox, reappeared with terrifying malignity during the Great Famine, their impact compounded by the presence of other infections, especially tuberculosis, rheumatic fever, bronchitis, influenza, pneumonia, scarlatina, diarrhoea and measles. According to one medical practitioner, these diseases had seldom been witnessed in the same intensity before.[10] To add to the physical and mental trauma of the poor, the dreaded "Asiatic cholera" appeared pandemically in 1848-49. To the beleaguered Irish, it must indeed have seemed as if the hand of Providence were raised against them.

"Fever" appears to have been a feature of the country for hundreds of years. Twelfth century visitors commented on its prevalence, as did Gerald Boate, during the Cromwellian wars. Boate called it malignant fever and said it was "commonly accompanied with a great pain in the head and in all the bones, great weakness, drought, loss of all manner of appetite, and want of sleep, and for the most part idleness or raving, and restlessness or tossings, but no very great nor constant heat".[11] In later centuries, fever was described by one medical commentator as the country's "scourge and chief destroyer", by another as its "great element of destruction".[12] Eighteenth and nineteenth century doctors did not know how the disease originated. Some contended that famine was the sole or paramount cause,[13] others that food shortage was only one of the agents involved. Other possible precipitating factors were the endemic poverty of the country, the wretched housing of the poor, their lack of clothing and fuel, dirt, depression, and intoxication, not to mention the pig in the kitchen and the middens that disgraced the frontage of every cabin in the country.[14]

Some Irish medical practitioners argued in favour of an extra-terrestrial agency. They suggested that the country's recurring outbreaks of fever were the result of some unknown connection between atmospheric or electrical phenomena and the generation of disease, the so-called "epidemic constitution".[15]

It is now known that the vector of "fever" was neither famine nor social distress, still less atmospheric abnormalities, but *pediculus humanus,* the human body louse. It is also known that there were two distinct but symptomatically related infections involved, typhus fever and relapsing fever. The epidemiology of the two diseases is very similar. Both are caused by micro-organisms, transmitted by lice. The typhus infection can enter the body through scratches on the skin, through the conjunctiva, or by inhalation, while relapsing fever is generally contracted through the skin. Typhus symptoms include high fever, prostration, mental confusion, body aches and a characteristic rash which covers the trunk and limbs of the body. In cases which are not going to recover, death usually occurs from heart failure about the fourteenth day.

Dr. Pemberton of Ballinrobe reported in 1848 that the first typhus symptoms of which people complained were a chilliness and a wish to be near the fire, or a severe rigor, accompanied by a dull, aching pain in the head. Sometimes his patients experienced lassitude and great weakness, intense pains in the loins and lower extremities, a furred tongue, quick pulse, hot skin, suffusion of the eyes, and flushed countenance. After a few days, delirium set in, with constant talking, of a low, muttering kind. In some cases, especially among the higher social classes, the talking was loud and boisterous. Petechiae were invariably present. They were barely detectable in some patients but others were covered from head to foot, with dark, almost black, spots, which were often as large as a four-penny piece.[16]

The features of relapsing fever are high temperature, generalised aches and pains, nausea, vomiting, nose bleeding and jaundice. In cases with a favourable outcome, the fever ends after five or six days with a sharp crisis attended by profuse sweating and exhaustion. This drop in body temperature was colloquially known as "getting the cool". The symptoms return after about a week and there may be several such relapses before the disease runs its course.[17] Some of Dr. Pemberton's patients experienced pains of such intensity in the back and joints, particularly in the ankle-joints, that they cried out whenever they stirred in bed.[18]

During the Great Famine, typhus fever prevailed in some parts of the country, relapsing fever in others. In certain districts the primary disease changed from typhus to relapsing fever and back again to typhus. Elsewhere, the two conspired together as "famine fever". No part of the country was immune, although some areas were more seriously affected than others. Relapsing fever was the prevalent disease among the general population, while the higher social classes tended to contract the more deadly typhus fever, especially those who were most exposed to infection, notably clergymen, doctors, members of relief committees and those connected with the administration of the poor law. The mortality rate from typhus was also more pronounced among the middle and upper classes than it was among the poor, who may have developed some immunity through long-term exposure to the disease.

The relationship between famine and fever is complex, but there is no direct nutritional connection. Increased vagrancy and mendicity, as well as overcrowding and the neglect of personal and domestic hygiene, all of them features of famine, created the optimum social conditions for lice infestation. Famine in Ireland invariably set a migratory chain in motion. The failure of the staple food of the poor encouraged or compelled many to abandon their useless potato gardens and to flee to cities and towns, as well as to seaports, to await transportation to a new life elsewhere. Increased itinerancy was largely responsible for diffusing fever throughout the country.

During the Great Famine, infected lice feasted on the unwashed and susceptible skin of the hungry, multiplied in their filthy and tattered clothing, and went forth, carried the length and breadth of the country by a population who had taken to the roads, vagrants and beggars, as well as the evicted and those who had abandoned their homes voluntarily. Lice found new and unresisting hosts at food depots and relief works, at social and religious gatherings, and in many public institutions, such as prisons and workhouses.

The general acceptance of the contagiousness of fever led to the establishment of fever hospitals, in which the infected could be isolated. About 100 of these hospitals had been established by the time the Famine began. During epidemics, additional accommodation was provided in wooden sheds and tents, which were often pitched in the grounds of existing hospitals. However, many parts of the country were devoid of medical institutions of any description and in these areas the infected, when not abandoned to their own devises, were isolated as far as possible at home or quarantined in so-called "fever huts". These were wretched structures of mud or stone which were hastily thrown up

at the side of a road, the corner of a field, or the verge of a bog. Some were even more rudimentary, consisting of nothing more than straw and furze tied together and placed at an angle to the ditch. Domestic quarantine, which was variously inspired by family affection, the absence of hospitals or the fear of entering them, was resorted to by rich and poor alike, although one pre-Famine report from County Kilkenny suggests that the practice was most common among the class of "comfortable farmers".[19] In single-roomed dwellings, those affected with fever were placed at one end of the cabin, while the healthy attempted to ward off infection as best they could at the other. In more substantial dwellings, the practice was to isolate the infected in a room by blocking up the door with sods. A hole was made in the rear wall, through which the medical attendant had to scramble on all fours.[20] Some doctors blamed the very high rate of mortality from fever among their colleagues on having to spend so much time in what one of them called "the wretched cabins of the poor".[21]

Reports from various parts of the country suggest that the first stage of relapsing fever was relatively mild. An account from Inishboffin stated that the initial attack was so slight that the afflicted "walked or rather staggered about with it".[22] A similar report from Dublin related that many passed through the fever "while they were literally walking about".[23] A characteristic of "famine fever" was the voracious hunger displayed by the patient after the attack had ended. "The hunger was in their hearts", said a nurse from Queen's County.[24] When the relapse occurred, it was invariably more prolonged and severe. A Co. Limerick doctor reported that "the relapsed stage was long, from ten to fourteen days, very severe, attended with great debility and prostration of strength".[25] These recurring bouts of fever further weakened an already debilitated population and left them very vulnerable to a host of other infections, such as dysentery, diarrhoea, cholera and smallpox.

The term "dysentery" was formerly applied to any condition in which inflammation of the colon was associated with the frequent passage of bloody stools. The term is now restricted to amoebic dysentery, which is almost entirely confined to tropical and sub-tropical countries, and to bacillary dysentery, an infectious disease which may occur sporadically or in epidemics. The disease is caused by the dysentery bacillus and the infection is spread by flies, by direct contact, or by pollution of the water by faeces infected with the bacillus.

Symptoms vary from a mild attack of diarrhoea to an acute fulminating infection. The duration of the diarrhoea varies from a few days to a fortnight, depending upon the severity of the attack.

A Cholera victim.

There may also be nausea, aching pain in the limbs, and shivery feelings, while there is always fever. An attack cannot develop except through the agency of the specific bacillus. However, anything which causes an intestinal upset, such as unsuitable food, predisposes to infection. Dysentery is rendered more virulent by famine and by the concurrence of other exhausting diseases. At one time, mortality rates were as high as 50 per cent during epidemics.[26]

During the terrible winter of 1846-47, chronic dysentery, or "starvation dysentery" as it was sometimes called, was very common, its prevalence attributed to the potato substitutes which the starving were compelled to eat, to the pickings of field, hedgerow and shoreline, and especially to the immoderate consumption of raw or partially cooked Indian meal by individuals who had neither the knowledge, firing or restraint to prepare it properly.[27] Dr. Cullinan of Ennis, Co. Clare, reported that the disease was attended with considerable pain and with great debility and restlessness, often terminating in chronic diarrhoea.

The onset was generally quite sudden. Within a few hours, a patient would have twelve or twenty alvine evacuations, consisting of a serous bloody fluid, often without a trace of mucus or faecal matter. "Sometimes the redder and more substantial portion would subside and present the appearance of a dark red, uncoagulated, homogeneous, viscid mass at the bottom of the vessel", he noted graphically.[28] Dr. Jones Lamprey of Schull, in west Cork, observed that the dejecta consisted mostly of "pure blood and mucus", adding that it was easy to detect those who were suffering from the disease as the floors and surrounds of their cabins were usually marked with clots of blood.[29] A colleague in nearby Skibbereen noted that the smell from evacuations was very offensive, almost intolerable and was similar to that of "putrid flesh in hot weather".[30] Another in Cork city commented on the "loathsome, putrid smell" that surrounded the diseased, as if, he said, "the decomposition of the vital organs had anticipated death".[31]

Dysentery is strongly conditioned by nutritional status but smallpox is so virulent that it acts independently of nutrition. The disease, which appeared epidemically in a very malignant form during the Famine, is no longer an active infection. It was an acute viral disease which was generally transmitted by airborne droplets. The characteristics of smallpox were high fever, headache, pain in the back and muscles, and occasionally in children vomiting and convulsions. In the severest infections, extreme toxaemia and massive haemorrhaging into the skin, lungs and other organs could cause death very quickly. Those who survived the attack were invariably left with a pocked and scarred face. Blindness was a possible consequence, as was infertility in males.[32]

Smallpox and fever terrified early and mid-nineteenth century Irish society. So did "Asiatic cholera", an acute diarrhoeal disease usually accompanied by vomiting and resulting in severe dehydration. The disease is caused by the *Vibrio cholerae* bacterium and is solely spread by infected humans, whose excreta may contaminate drinking water and food.[33] Asiatic or epidemic cholera was not one of the fevers of the Great Famine. Its appearance was coincidental but it added to the general distress and mortality. Cholera spread pandemically from India at various times in the nineteenth century, most spectacularly in the early 1830s, when it caused great consternation in Ireland and elsewhere. The disease reappeared late in the following decade. The first case recorded in Ireland occurred at Belfast on 4th December 1848, the last exactly twenty months later. During this period, a total of 45,698 cases were reported to the Central Board of Health, of which 19,325 proved fatal. This represents a mortality rate of 42.3 per cent.[34]

William Wilde regarded the board of health figures as an underestimate for the country as a whole and in the 1851 census attributed 35,989 deaths to the disease.[35] However, Wilde's returns are also unreliable, as he conflated cholera and some dysentery and diarrhoea mortality. This is an indication of the circumspection with which the 1851 census needs to be approached.[36] A similar caveat applies to Irish records generally before 1864, the year in which compulsory notification of death was introduced. Before then, medical practitioners, hospitals, and other institutions, if they kept records at all, did so irregularly and idiosyncratically. In addition, diagnosis and disease classification were often vague and inconsistent.

The Great Famine magnified these difficulties. Those who were entrusted with the lives of the starving are unlikely to have been overly concerned with statistical niceties. In the circumstances, it was almost inevitable that there should have been considerable institutional and administrative error and confusion.[37] Thus, analysis of morbidity and mortality rates for starvation, deficiency diseases and infection during the Great Famine poses many difficulties. At this stage, all we can say with any certainty is that more than 1,000,000 people died of hunger and disease in Ireland in the late 1840s.[38] This was an obscenity, searing testimony of the degradation, distress and terror experienced by our forebears. As ever, during famine, it was the most vulnerable in society, the young, the old, the poor and the sick, who suffered most. ▨

References

1. Samuel Edge, MD, Queen's County, to Sir Philip Crampton, Central Board of Health, Dublin, 18 February 1847, CSORP 1847 H 3420 National Archives of Ireland.
2. The foregoing section on the biological, psychological and social effects of starvation is derived from Robert Dirks, 'Famine and disease', in *The Cambridge world history of human disease* (Cambridge: Cambridge University Press, 1993), pp. 157-160.
3. Daniel Donovan, 'Observations on the peculiar diseases to which the famine of last year gave origin, and on the morbid effects of insufficient nourishment', *Dublin Medical Press*, 2 February, 1 March, 3 May 1848 pp. 67-8, 129-132, 275-8.
4. Ibid., 9 August 1848, pp. 84-6.
5. *Dublin Quarterly Journal of Medical Science*, 7(1849), p. 401.
6. Myron Winick, ed., 'Hunger disease: studies by the Jewish physicians in the Warsaw ghetto', *Nutrition*, 10(1994), pp. 365-380.
7. *Dublin Quarterly Journal of Medical Science*, 8(1849), pp. 281-2.
8. William A. R. Thomson, ed., *Black's medical dictionary* (London: Adam & Charles Black, 34th ed., 1984), pp. 794-5; E. Margaret Crawford, 'Scurvy in Ireland during the Great Famine', *Social History of Medicine*, 1(1988), pp. 281-300; Idem, 'Subsistence crises and famines in Ireland', in E. Margaret Crawford, ed., *Famine: the Irish experience, 900-1900. Subsistence crises and famines in Ireland* (Edinburgh: John Donald, 1989), pp. 207-214; Idem, 'Dearth, diet and disease in Ireland, 1850: a case study of nutritional deficiency', *Medical History*, 28(1984), pp. 151-161; Idem, 'Indian meal and pellagra in nineteenth century Ireland', in J. M. Goldstrom and L. A. Clarkson, *Irish population, economy and society; Essays in honour of the late K. H. Connell* (Oxford, 1981), pp. 113-133.
9. Dirks, 'Famine and disease', pp. 160-1.
10. *Dublin Medical Press*, 9 August 1848, p. 84.
11. Charles Creighton, *A history of epidemics in Britain* (Cambridge: Cambridge University Press, 2 vols, 1894), 2, pp. 224-234.
12. John O' Brien, 'Medical report of the house of recovery, and fever hospital, Cork Street, Dublin, for the year ending 4th of January, 1827', *Transactions of the Association of Fellows and Licentiates of the King and Queen's College of Physicians in Ireland*, v(1828), p. 512; William Wilde, in *The census of Ireland for the year 1851*, Part V, Tables of deaths, vol. 1, Brit. Parl. Papers 1856[2087-1], xxix, p. 246.
13. See, for instance, D. J. Corrigan, *On famine and fever as cause and effect in Ireland; with observations on hospital location, and the dispensation in outdoor relief of food and medicine* (Dublin: J. Fannin, 1846), pp. 1-33.
14. See, for instance, *First report of the General Board of Health* (Dublin, 1822), p. 118; Poor inquiry (Ireland). Appendix B, containing general reports upon the existing system of public medical relief in Ireland; local reports upon dispensaries, fever hospitals, county infirmaries and lunatic asylums; with supplement, parts 1 and 2, containing answers to questions from the officers etc. of medical institutions, *Brit. Par. Papers*, 1835 (369) xxxii, part 2, supplement, pp. 1-262.

15. Henry Kennedy, *Observations on the connexion between famine and fever in Ireland, and elsewhere* (Dublin: Hodges and Smith, 1847), pp. 43-8; *Dublin Quarterly Journal of Medical Science*, 7(1849), p. 92; Robert James Graves, *A system of clinical medicine* (Dublin: Fannin, 1843), pp. 41-2, 45.
16. *Dublin Quarterly Journal of Medical Science*, 7(1849), pp. 370-1.
17. *Black's medical dictionary*, pp. 758-9, 920; William P. MacArthur, 'Medical history of the famine', in R. Dudley Edwards and T. Desmond Williams, eds, *The great famine: studies in Irish history, 1845-52* (New York: New York University Press, 1957; reprinted Dublin: Lilliput Press, 1994), pp. 265-8; William O' Brien, 'The fevers of the great famine', *Journal of the Irish Colleges of Physicians and Surgeons*, 10 (July 1980), pp. 46-9; John D. Post, *Food shortage, climatic variability, and epidemic disease in pre industrial Europe. The mortality peak in the early 1740s* (Ithaca and London: Cornell University Press, 1985), pp. 228-233.
18. *Dublin Quarterly Journal of Medical Science*, 7(1849), pp. 372-3.
19. *Dublin Medical Press*, 22 May 1844, p. 325.
20. Ibid. See also, a report from Cappawhite, County Tipperary, June 1846, CSORP 1846 H 10916, National Archives of Ireland (Hereafter NAI), and the evidence of Francis Burges, Fethard, County Tipperary, OP 1849/63, NAI.
21. OP 1849/63, NAI. See Laurence M. Geary, 'The Great Famine and the Fethard temporary fever hospital', in *Tipperary Historical Journal* (forthcoming, 1997)
22. *Dublin Quarterly Journal of Medical Science*, 7(1849), pp. 378-9.
23. Ibid., 8(1849), p. 50.
24. Ibid., p. 42.
25. Ibid., 7(1849), p. 73.
26. *Black's medical dictionary*, pp. 290-2; MacArthur, 'Medical history of the famine', pp. 268-9.
27. *Dublin Quarterly Journal of Medical Science*, 7(1849), pp. 103-4.
28. Ibid., p. 91.
29. Ibid., p. 104.
30. *Dublin Medical Press*, 3 May 1848, p. 276. See also, Ibid., 17 November 1847, pp. 306-7.
31. *Dublin Quarterly Journal of Medical Science*, 8(1849), p. 281.
32. Alfred W. Crosby, 'Smallpox', in *The Cambridge world history of human disease*, pp. 1008-9.
33. Reinhard S. Speck, 'Cholera', in Ibid., pp. 642-3.
34. *Report of the commissioners of health, Ireland, on the epidemics of 1846 to 1850* (Dublin, 1852), pp. 28-42
35. *The census of Ireland for the year 1851*, Part V, Tables of deaths, vol. 1, Brit. Parl. Papers 1856[2087-1], xxix, pp. 251-2.
36. The inadequacies of the 1851 census have long been recognised by historians. See, for instance, P. Froggatt, 'Sir William Wilde and the 1851 census of Ireland', *Medical History*, 9(1965), pp. 302-26.
37. See, for instance, *Dublin Quarterly Journal of Medical Science*, 7(1849), p. 117.
38. Joel Mokyr, *Why Ireland starved: a quantitative and analytical history of the Irish economy, 1800-1850* (London: George Allen & Unwin, 1985), pp. 263-8; Cormac Ó Gráda, *Ireland. A new economic history, 1780-1939* (Oxford: Clarendon Press, 1994), pp. 178-187.

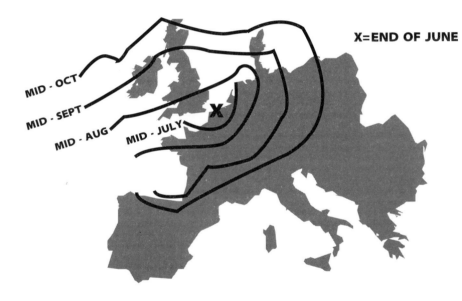

THE POTATO FAMINE IN EUROPE

Peter M. Solar

The potato blight struck the whole of Europe in the late 1840s. As Austin Bourke's[1] pioneering research has shown, blight seems to have arrived from the United States in 1844 with a shipment of seed potatoes offloaded at Ostende in Belgium. No serious damage was caused that year but the disease spread rapidly throughout the continent in the latter half of 1845 and again in 1846. Although yields everywhere were adversely affected there was *no* potato famine in Europe, certainly nothing on the same scale as the Irish catastrophe.

It is true that in the late 1840s economic conditions on the continent were difficult: 1846, 1847 and 1848 were particularly troubled. But there is little question of a potato famine. Instead, continental historians speak of a *crise agraire* or an Agrarkrise in which potato crop failure was only one element.[2,3] Or they refer to a more general economic crisis affecting commerce and industry as well as agriculture and playing a role in the political upheavals of 1848.[4,5] The interaction between blight and these other economic factors helps to explain the incidence of distress on the continent. Their impact on Ireland has often been overlooked in discussions of the famine.

Although many people in Europe went hungry in the late 1840's, there were remarkably few signs of potato famine, or of famine of any sort, at least in the life-threatening sense. Death rates were almost everywhere a bit higher in the late 1840s than in the early 1840s. This was especially true in 1847 and 1848 when cholera epidemics broke out in various parts of Europe. But nowhere in Europe experienced catastrophic mortality rates like those in Ireland.[6,7] One question to be explained is why famine did not prevail outside Ireland, why a book entitled *The Last Great Subsistence Crisis in the Western World* deals with the years from 1816 to 1819 and not with those from 1846 to 1849.[8]

The potato-growing regions of Europe

The blight could have had a major impact only where potatoes were grown in significant quantities, so the stage must be set by looking at the incidence of potato cultivation in Europe. The limits of European agricultural statistics before the late- nineteenth century make it impossible to do this with any pretence at precision or comprehensiveness but it is possible to obtain a rough and ready idea of where potatoes may have accounted for more than, say, 10 per cent of the acreage under crops.

One concentration, close to Ireland, took in much of Scotland: not only the Highlands but also lowland areas stretching from south of Glasgow to Dundee.[9] This area also extended down into northwestern England, where potato growing was a distinctive feature of agriculture in Lancashire and Cheshire.[10,11] Another concentration covered much of Belgium and the Netherlands, along with some adjoining areas of Germany.[12,13] Further south, potatoes were an important crop along the Franco-German border, in Alsace, the Rhineland and Baden-Wurttemburg, and on into northern Switzerland.[14,15,16,17] In alpine regions of Switzerland, Italy and Austria, potatoes were often the major crop.[18,19]

Further east another concentration lay along the border between Prussia and Austria: in parts of Saxony, Silesia, Bohemia and Austrian Galicia.[20,21] Potatoes were also widely cultivated in eastern Poland, parts of White Russia, and the Baltic provinces.[22,23] Other pockets of relatively intensive cultivation were scattered across Europe: in Brittany, in parts of the Massif Central and the Pyrenees; in Spanish Galicia; in parts of Denmark, Norway and Sweden.[24,25,26,27,28]

Although potato cultivation was important in many areas of northern Europe, it is worth noting at the outset that 10 per cent of the cropped land was, by Irish standards, not very much. Very few European regions had more than 15 per cent of their cultivated land under potatoes; the likely candidates were parts of Scotland, Flanders, Holland and Alsace, and some Alpine regions.

Few Irish counties, by contrast, had less than 20 per cent. For Ireland as a whole, almost a third of all the land under crops, meadow and clover was devoted to the potato.[29] Only in a few parts of Scotland and Switzerland does the potato appear to have played such a prominent role. One reason, then, why blight-induced famine is hard to find outside Ireland is simply that there were fewer potatoes to be infested.

Some potato-growing parts of Europe were also less vulnerable because a large share of the crop went to uses other than direct human consumption. In eastern Europe and Scandinavia enormous quantities were made into alcohol. In 1846 contemporaries estimated that 25 per cent of the crop in Bohemia and 40 per cent in Galicia was distilled.[30] In Western Europe a large share of the crop - perhaps half in Belgium - was fed to pigs.[31]

Once these and other uses, such as starch and syrup-making, were taken into account, contemporaries often reckoned that less than half of the net crop was eaten directly. This meant that most European regions had a somewhat larger buffer against famine than was the case in Ireland, where almost 60 per cent of the crop went directly for human consumption.[32]

Some patterns may be detected in these concentrations of potato cultivation in Europe. One is the prominence of upland areas: the Alps, the Pyrenees, the Scottish Highlands, Spanish Galicia, the Vosges and the Black Forest, the Erzebirge, and the Sudeten and Carpathian Mountains along the Czech-German and Czech-Polish borders. In many of these places cold and wet spells during the growing season made reliance on cereal crops precarious. Potatoes were a sturdier crop in such conditions and were widely adopted.

In upland districts of the Swiss canton of Bern, for example, between a third and two-thirds of the cultivated land was under potatoes in the 1840s.[33] In upland areas potatoes were typically cultivated by smallholders and used primarily for their own consumption.

But potatoes were also cultivated extensively in lowland areas. In some of these areas much of the crop was sold off-farm in one form or another. Potato growing had a more commercial aspect and took place on larger farms.

In parts of Lancashire and Cheshire some farmers produced two crops a year for sale in the Manchester and Liverpool markets, sprouting early potatoes inside before transplanting them to the fields.[34] In the Dutch provinces of Friesland and Holland farmers sold their potatoes to urban markets and to distilleries and starch works.[35]

In Poland increased commercial production during the 1820s and 1830s took place mainly on the lords', as against the serfs', land. The lords turned the crop into a flood of vodka: in the 1840s consumption was three gallons of 100 per cent spirit yearly per head, women and children included, which was about six times Poland's mid-twentieth century consumption.[36]

Yet not all lowland areas were dominated by commercial producers. In Flanders, parts of the Netherlands, and the Rhineland, most of the potato crop was produced on smaller holdings and consumed on the farm.

Another characteristic of Europe's potato-growing regions is the way in which they overlap with areas of textile, and especially of linen textile, production.[37] The fit is not perfect. There were linen-producing areas where potato cultivation was not extensive: much of northern France and parts of central Germany. Similarly, there were potato-growing areas without a textile tradition, such as the Belgian province of Luxemburg and parts of Poland.

But most major centres of linen textile production were characterised by extensive potato cultivation. This was the case in lowland Scotland, Flanders, Bohemia and Silesia. Other potato-growing regions, such as Lancashire, Alsace and parts of Switzerland, had been linen regions before going over to cotton production in the late eighteenth and early nineteenth centuries.

The nexus between linen and potatoes is the farmer-weaver and, perhaps even more importantly, his spinner-wife. The linen industry was the one textile industry in which, with only a limited amount of land, the weaver could supply his own raw material.

As field crops, potatoes and flax went together for several reasons. They were complementary crops in that their peak labour demands occurred at different times of the year. They could both make use of family labour, especially in weeding and harvesting. Relative to cereals, they yielded high value per acre, which permitted the intensification of production on small holdings. Preparing of flax and its spinning by hand provided further outlets for family labour, especially in the slack winter months.[38]

This farmer-weaver nexus had all but disappeared by the 1840s in some textile areas, notably in Lancashire and lowland Scotland.

But it might be conjectured that commercial production of potatoes in these areas reflected urban demand shaped by the descendants of farmer-weavers.

The effects of blight on European potato crops

In examining where in Europe potatoes were extensively cultivated and by looking at the economic characteristics of these areas, the stage has been set. Now, enter the villain: *Phytophthora infestans*, stealthy, lethal, capricious, ever present, no respecter of persons or borders.

Bourke's (1993) careful research has shown that in 1845 the impact of the blight depended on the distance from its epicentre in Belgium. In the Low Countries crops were devastated: in Belgium 90 per cent of the crop was lost; in the northern Dutch province of Groningen, 75 per cent.[39,40] In northern France, western parts of Germany, and southern England a quarter to a half of the crop was lost.[41] Elsewhere, as in much of Ireland, the disease arrived toward the end of the growing season, after the tubers had been formed, so the reduction in yields was not so severe.

By the summer of 1846 the blight had become endemic and its impact took on a different pattern. The crops in the Low Countries were again devastated. So, too, were crops in northern England and Scotland; in Prussia, where yields were down by a half or more,[42,43] in Bohemia and Austrian Galicia, where yields were only a fourth to a fifth of normal.[44]

In southeast England, France and southern Germany, by contrast, the fall in yields seems to have been less severe, perhaps because the warm, dry summer was uncongenial to blight in these areas.

During subsequent years the blight became more capricious. The 1847 crop seems to have been reasonably good in the Netherlands and France, but poor in Prussia. In 1848 the situation was just the reverse.[45] In these years there were only sporadic outbreaks in Lancashire.

The impact of the blight on European potato crops was thus most severe and most widespread in 1846, though the effects of the first outbreak in 1845 should not be neglected. These unprecedented and extremely severe shortfalls of production were the blight's contribution to the more general crisis of the late 1840s.

The blight had a longer-term impact on European agriculture. Its intermittent outbreaks reduced average potato yields and made potato growing a much riskier activity. The longer-term effects can be readily seen in prices. The prices of potatoes relative to those of cereals were, on average, 50-100 per cent higher in the late 1840s and 1850s than in the 1830s and early 1840s.[46] The blight was a large, negative and persistent productivity shock that reduced the returns to potato growing.

Other causes of the late 1840s crisis

Villainous though the blight may have been, there would not have been much drama on the European stage in the late 1840s without two other, perhaps more important, actors. One enters with a flourish, causes mayhem throughout Europe, then vanishes almost as quickly. The other was pushed from centre stage by blight, but, instead of disappearing, remained along with the blight to play out small tragedies in parts of Britain and the continent.

The first actor was drought, which appeared in the summer of 1846 and devastated European cereal crops. In France and Prussia wheat yields were 25 per cent below those of a normal year. The fall in rye yields in the Netherlands and Prussia was even larger, at about 40 per cent.[47,48] These were exceptionally large shortfalls for European cereal crops in the nineteenth century.[49]

The failure of the wheat and rye crops has usually taken precedence in discussions of the crisis in Europe during the late 1840s. This is only fair, since these crops still fed most Europeans. But the role of the potato crop failure has probably been understated for three reasons.

The first is purely arithmetic: even though bread was more important than potatoes in the European diet, the net deficiency in the cereal crop was only half that of the potato crop. Second, the cereal crop failures were all the more disastrous, given the unavailability of potatoes as an alternate foodstuff. During the early nineteenth century the cultivation of potatoes had served to diversify the European diet and, in so far as cereal and potato harvests failed at different times, to reduce the consequences of harvest failures.[50] The year 1846 was doubly unusual in that both crops failed catastrophically in the same year. A third reason for putting more weight on the blight's effects is that reserves of grain in Europe had probably been depleted in late 1845 and early 1846. As cereals were substituted for potatoes after the 1845 shortfalls, this reduced grain stocks and left the European economy more vulnerable to the 1846 failures. Drought wreaked havoc with European food supplies in 1846, then went away. In 1847 European cereal crops were particularly abundant: as unusually abundant as they had been deficient in 1846. Crops in the following years were also good, with the result that Europeans benefited from the lowest bread prices of the century in the last years of the 1840s. For those with the income to buy food the crisis was over in autumn 1847.

The other major actor in the drama of the late 1840s was structural change in industry. The mechanisation of industry in Britain and elsewhere in Europe was putting pressure on the incomes of rural households involved in domestic manufacturing.

The 1840s were a particularly difficult period for spinners and weavers of linen.[51] From the late 1820s, when the first wet-spinning factories were built in Leeds and Belfast, machine-made yarn had begun to displace hand spun. Improvements in machinery during the 1830s laid the groundwork for the large increase in the numbers of mechanical spindles that took place from the 1830s to the early 1850s. Handspinners on the continent suffered first from imports of machine-spun yarn from Britain and Ireland, then increasingly from the output of factories set up in Flanders, northern France, Silesia and Bohemia.[52]

The inexorable death of hand spinning put large numbers of women out of work. In Flanders there had been more than 200,000 hand spinners; there were similar numbers in Bohemia and Silesia.[53,54] As yarn prices fell, their contribution to household incomes slowly disappeared. The same thing happened in Ireland. Of the job losses in Irish manufacturing between 1841 and 1851 most were in the textile sector and within the textile sector these were primarily women spinners.[55,56]

Machine-made yarn gave no major impetus to the weaving of linen cloth, which itself was not mechanised until the 1850s and 1860s. At best, cheaper yarn allowed linen weavers only to hold their ground against competition from cotton textiles. Slow or no growth in output, together with an influx of women into weaving pushed down the rates paid to weavers, further depressing household incomes in linen-producing regions.[57,58]

Structural change in industry was not confined to the 1840s nor to the linen industry. Earlier, domestic workers in the cotton and woollen industries had been displaced by factory production. Later, handloom weavers of linen would lose out to the power loom. Even in the 1840s there were other expanding opportunities for rural women in still unmechanised occupations such as embroidery and lace-making.[59,60] But the changes taking place in the linen industry in the 1840s are important in understanding the incidence and the duration of the crisis arising from potato and cereal crop failures.

The incidence of distress

The parts of Europe which suffered most and longest during the late 1840s were those where potatoes were extensively grown and where a substantial linen industry existed. The prime examples were Flanders and the borderlands between Bohemia and Prussia, where death rates and destitution were high in 1846-47 and remained high for a few years thereafter.[61] Other cases may include Spanish Galicia and the Sarthe in France. Areas with linen but without too many potatoes, like the French Nord and parts of Westphalia, and areas with potatoes but no linen, like Alsace, lowland Switzerland and Lancashire, largely escaped acute crisis.[62]

The linen-potato nexus does not, of course, explain everything. Some exceptions are easy to deal with. One area which had both potatoes and linen, but suffered little, was eastern Scotland. The linen industry around Dundee was, however, unusual in that it was highly specialised on coarse fabrics, which faced less competition from cotton. The spinning of coarse yarn had also been mechanised much earlier, so that handspinning of linen had essentially disappeared from eastern Scotland by the 1840s.[63]

Among the areas with potatoes but no linen were a number of upland areas where there were indeed signs of persistent distress. The introduction of the blight undermined the viability of small holdings in the western highlands of Scotland and in the higher regions of the Alps and the Pyrenees. These were the few areas of Europe where reliance on potatoes was at all comparable to that in Ireland. Why their distress did not turn into catastrophe will be addressed later.

The most awkward exception to the linen-potato nexus is the Netherlands. The linen industry was not at all important in the parts of the country hit hardest by the blight, yet there is clear evidence of distress and excess mortality.[64] In order to explain the Dutch case and some of the other anomalies, two other factors which could either mitigate or exacerbate the impact of the blight need to be introduced.

One factor is the distribution of land and its relationship to the agricultural labour market. Where smallholders also owned their land, they had additional resources to help surmount the crisis. They could, if necessary, borrow against their property, or even sell out. In the longer term, if they had enough land, they could shift away from potatoes to other intensive crops. Where smallholders were tenants or only obtained land in exchange for labour, they were more vulnerable.

Where most land was on large holdings and farmers hired labourers for wages, the labourers' position was most precarious. In the short-term labourers faced rising food prices. In the longer term farmers might shift production away from potatoes, reducing the demand for their labour.

The other factor was the scale and efficacy of relief efforts. In mid-nineteenth century Europe national and local governments had only a limited capability for intervention, for want of resources and administrative capacity. Some governments, for ideological reasons, chose not to use what limited capabilities they did possess. Sometimes private charity could substitute for state intervention; sometimes it could not.

The Dutch case shows a particularly unpropitious configuration of these two additional elements.[65,66] Dutch agriculture, especially in the coastal provinces, was highly commercial. Farms were good-sized and the use of wage labour common. The blight hit labourers very hard, since they grew potatoes for their own consumption on small plots hired from farmers. Farmers also grew potatoes for urban markets and for distilling and starchmaking, but with the advent of blight (and freer access to the British market) they increasingly turned away from potato cultivation towards dairying.

The plight of the labourers in Friesland and other coastal provinces was not helped by the Dutch government's staunch refusal to intervene in markets, to distribute relief, or to undertake public works. The national government went even further by actively preventing local authorities from taking action, choosing to rely on the country's well-developed charitable institutions. Private charity was reasonably effective in 1845-46, but not sufficient to deal with the crisis of 1846-47. In the longer term the decline of potato cultivation left pockets of persistent poverty, notably in Friesland.

The Scottish highlands present another configuration of these factors.[67,68] Here the structure of landholding - predominantly small tenancies - was unfavourable, but the relief effort, both public and private, was largely effective in preventing a significant rise in death rates in the late 1840s. The longer term impact of the blight was increased emigration and population decline.

In Flanders, by contrast with the Netherlands, determined public and private relief efforts helped mitigate what was probably a more significant problem.[69,70] Landownership was also more widely dispersed than in the Netherlands and Scotland. Farmer-weavers generally managed to cling to their land, which may have helped in the short run. Over the longer term many of these holdings were no longer viable and rural poverty was endemic in Flanders until this century.

In Germany and Bohemia land ownership was also widely dispersed in most potato-growing regions. Holdings were typically larger than in Flanders, so property ownership probably played a larger role in limiting distress than did relief efforts, which do not appear to have been either large or well organised.[71]

The Irish Famine in the European mirror

This interpretation of the blight's short-and long-term impact in Europe has stressed its interaction with cereal crop failures in 1846 and with structural changes in industry. The structures of land ownership and occupation and government relief policies also played important roles. How does the Irish experience look from this European perspective?

Ireland during the late 1840s looks like a collage of several parts of Europe. With its small farms and domestic manufacturing, the linen belt stretching from Antrim and Down westward towards parts of Sligo and Mayo looks like Flanders or the Bohemian-Silesian borderland. Within Ireland, Ulster suffered least from blight's effects; on the continent Bohemia was perhaps hardest hit. Here the differences between Ireland and the rest of Europe were least pronounced.

The west and southwest of Ireland resemble the western isles and highlands of Scotland, without generous relief, or the high Alpine valleys and Spanish Galicia, without dispersed land ownership. These were areas where dense settlement could be sustained only with a high-yielding and reliable potato. The blight rendered them unviable. Relief or the ownership of some land eased the transition in the rest of Europe. No such factor did so in the west of Ireland.

The east, and especially the southeast, of Ireland is a more puzzling area. Some of the highest concentrations of potato growing - over 30 per cent of the cultivated land - were to be found in the fertile counties of Carlow, Wexford, Waterford, Kilkenny and Tipperary. Here commercial farmers using hired labour were feeding animals with potatoes to produce butter and bacon for the British market.

This part of Ireland looks like parts of the Netherlands, a comparison first made several years ago by Joel Mokyr.[72] But where Mokyr stressed the two countries' common failure to industrialise, the extent to which agriculture was commercialised seems to be the common feature of importance.

These comparisons with experience in the rest of Europe suggest that the impact of the blight in Ireland needs to be seen through the prism of local economic and social structures. But a continental perspective also prompts two more general remarks about the Irish experience. The first is that relief efforts mattered.

The resources of the nineteenth century state were not unlimited but, if mobilised, they could help relieve distress and keep down mortality. Here the success of relief in the Scottish Highlands and Western Isles and the contrast between interventionist Belgium and laissez-faire Holland are pertinent. The second remark, which qualifies the first, is that in the short run the impact of the cereal crop failures of 1846 should not be overlooked. Although in Ireland the wheat crop was of secondary importance, and the rye crop of no importance at all, their failure on the contintent was crucial. In late

1846 and early 1847 everyone was looking for grain supplies, and several countries were restricting exports of cereals. Consumers and relief authorities in all countries, including Ireland, thus faced the grave reality that both of northern Europe's major sources of nutrition - cereals and potatoes - would be catastrophically short in the same year. ▧

NOTE:

I am grateful to Karl Ditt, Giovanni Federico, Cormac Ó Gráda, James Simpson, Johan Soderberg and Jan van Zanden, without the benefit of whose advice on the existing literature this interpretative essay would have been impossible.

References

1. P. M.A. Bourke, (1993). *'The Visitation of God'? The Potato and the Great Irish Famine*, Dublin.
2. G. Duby and A. Wallon, (1976). *Histoire de la France rurale. 3. De 1789 a 1914*, Paris.
3. W. Abel, (1980). *Agricultural Fluctuations in Europe*, London.
4. M. Bergman,1967. The Potato Blight in the Netherlands and its Social Consequences (1845-1847). *International Review of Social History* 17: 390-431.
5. M. Gailus, (1994). Food Riots in Germany in the Late 1840s. *Past and Present*, No. 145, pp. 156-193.
6. W. R. Lee, (1979). *European Demography and Economic Growth*, London.
7. J.L. Van Zanden, (1990). Den zedenlijken en materielen toestand der arbeidende bevolking ten platten lande. *Een reeks repporten uit 1851*, Groningen.
8. J. Post, (1977). *The Last Great Subsistence Crisis in the Western World*, Baltimore.
9. R. Salaman, (1949). *The History and Social Influence of the Potato*, Cambridge.
10. R. Salaman, (1949).Op. cit.
11. J. Caird, (1852). *English Agriculture in 1850-51*, London.
12. M. Goossens,(1992). *The Economic Development of Belgian Agriculture: A Regional Perspective, 1812-1846*, Brussels.
13. J.L.Van Zanden,. (1985). *De economische ontwikkeling van de nederlandse landbouw in de negentiende eeuw, 1800-1914*, Utrecht.
14. H. Clout, (1980). *Agriculture in France on the Eve of the Railway Age*, London.
15. J. Blum, (1978). *The End of the Old Order in Rural Europe*, Princeton.
16. Anne-Lise Head-Konig, L. Hubler, and C. Pfister, 1987. Evolution agraire et demographique en Suisse (XVIIe-XIXe siecles). In: *Evolution agraire et croissance demographique (ed.* Antoinette Fauve-Chamoux), Liege, pp. 233-261.
17. C. Pfister, (1990). Food Supply in the Swiss Canton of Bern, 1850. In: *Hunger in History* (ed. Newman, L.F.), Oxford, pp. 281-303.
18. P.P. Viazzo, (1989). *Upland Communities: Environment, Population and Social Structure in the Alps since the Sixteenth Century*, Cambridge.
19. R. Sandgruber, (1978). *Oesterreichische Agrarstatistik, 1750-1918*, Munchen.
20. J. Blum, (1978). *op. cit.*
21. R. Sandgruber, (1978). *Oesterreichische Agrarstatistik, 1750-1918*, Munchen.
22. J. Blum, (1978). *op. cit.*
23. S. Kieniewicz, (1969). *The Emancipation of the Polish Peasantry*, Chicago.
24. H. Clout, (1980). *Agriculture in France on the Eve of the Railway Age*, London
25. A. Bouhier, (1979). *La Galice: essai geographique d'analyse et d'interpretation d'un vieux complexe agraire*, La Roche-sur-Yon.
26. Rodriguez Galdo, M.X. and F. Dopico, (1981). *Crisis agrarias y crecimiento economico en Galicia en el siglo XIX*, La Coruna.
27. M. Drake, (1969). *Population and Society in Norway 1735-1865*, Cambridge.
28. G. Fridlizius, (1984). The Mortality Decline in the Fist Phase of the Demographic Transition: Swedish Experiences. In: *Pre-Industrial Population Change* (eds. Bengtsson, T., Fridlizius, G. and Ohlsson, R.), Stockholm, pp. 71-114.

29. J. Mokyr, (1981). Irish History with the Potato. *Irish Economic and Social History* 8: 8-29.
30. J. Blum, (1978). *The End of the Old Order in Rural Europe*, Princeton. pp. 296.
31. M. Goossens, (1992). *The Economic Development of Belgian Agriculture Regional Perspective, 1812-1846*, Brussels. pp. 139.
32. P.M. Solar, (1989). The Great Famine was no Ordinary Subsistence Crisis. In: *Famine: The Irish Experience 900-1900* (ed. Crawford, E.M.), Edinburgh, pp.112-33.
33. P.P. Viazzo, (1989). *Upland Communities: Environment, Population and Social Structure in the Alps since the Sixteenth Century*, Cambridge. pp. 212-3.
34. R. Scola, (1992). *Feeding the Victorian City: The Food Supply of Manchester, 1770-1870*, Manchester.
35. J. Bieleman, (1992). *Geschiedenis van de landbouw in Nederland 1500-1950*, Amsterdam.
36. S. Kieniewicz, (1969). *The Emancipation of the Polish Peasantry*, Chicago. pp. 90-1.
37. P.M. Solar, In press. The European Linen Industry, 1780-1914. Forthcoming in: *The Cambridge History of Western Textiles* (eds. Jenkins, D.T. and Harte, N.), Cambridge.
38. W. Mager, (1993). *Proto-Industrialisation and Proto-Industry: the Uses and Drawbacks of Two Concepts, Continuity and Change*, pp. 8, 2, 181-215.
39. G. Jacquemyns, (1929). *Histoire de la crise economique des Flandres (1845-1850)*, Brussels.
40. P. Priester, (1991). *De economische ontwikkeling van de landbouw in Groningen 1800-1910*, Wageningen.
41. P.M.A. Bourke, (1993). *'The Visitation of God'? The Potato and the Great Irish Famine*, Dublin.
42. K. Obermann, (1972). Wirtschafts- und sozialpolitische Aspekte der Krise von 1845-1847 in Deutschland, insbesondere in Preussen. *Jahrbuch fur Geschichte* 7: 141-174.
43. J. Bergmann, (1979). Oekonomische Voraussetzungen der Revolution von 1848. Zur Krise von 1845 bis 1848 in Deutschland. In: Jurgen Bergmann, Klaus Megerle and Peter Steinbach, *Geschichte als politische Wissenschaft*, Stuttgart, pp. 24-54.
44. R. Sandgruber, (1978). *Oesterreichische Agrarstatistik, 1750-1918*, Munchen.
45. K. Obermann, (1972). *op. cit.*
46. P.M. Solar, (1989). The Great Famine was no Ordinary Subsistence Crisis. In: *Famine: The Irish Experience 900-1900* (ed. Crawford, E.M.), Edinburgh, pp.112-33
47. K. Obermann, (1972). *op. cit.*
48. P. Priester, (1991). *De economische ontwikkeling van de landbouw in Groningen 1800-1910*, Wageningen.
49. P.M. Solar, (1989). The Great Famine. *op. cit.*
50. M. Drake, (1969). *Population and Society in Norway*, Cambridge.
51. G. Jacquemyns, (1929). *Histoire de la crise economique des Flandres (1845-1850)*, Brussels.
52. P. M. Solar, (1992). Die belgische Leinenindustrie im 19. Jahrhundert. In: *Industrialisierung und Arbeiterschaft in Leinen - und Baumwollregionen West - und Mitteleuropas* (eds. Ditt, K. and Pollard, S.), Paderborn, pp. 78- 105

53. G. Jacquemyns, (1929). *op. cit.*
54. P.M. Solar, The European Linen Industry.
55. UK Parliamentary Papers. 1843. *Reports of the Commissioners Appointed to Take the Census of Ireland for the Year 1841,* vol. XXIV.
56. UK Parliamentary Papers. 1856. *The Census of Ireland for the Year 1851,* vol. XXXI.
57. P.M. Solar, (1990). The Irish Linen Trade, 1820-1852. *Textile History* **21:** 57-85.
58. P.M. Solar, (1992). Die belgische Leinenindustrie im 19. *op. cit.*
59. B. Collins, (1992). Die Heimarbeiterschaft im Leinengewerbe Ulsters wahrend des 19. und 20. Jahrhunderts. In: *Industrialisierung und Arbeiterschaft in Leinen- und Baumwollregionen West - und Mitteleuropas* (eds. Ditt, K. and Pollard, S.), Paderborn, pp. 232-258.
60. E. Gubin, and P. Scholliers, (1992). Die Mechanisierung des Flachsspinnens in Flandern: Landliche Heimarbeiter und industrielles Proletariat (1840-1900). In: *Industrialisierung und Arbeiterschaft in Leinen - und Baumwollregionen West - und Mitteleuropas* (eds. Ditt, K. and Pollard, S.), Paderborn, pp. 259-289.
61. B. Bolognese-Leuchtenmuller, (1978). *Bevolkerungsentwicklung und Berufsstruktur, Gesundheits- und Fursorgewesen in Oesterreich 1750-1918,* Munchen.
62. F.G. Dreyfus, (1956). La crise dans un department de l'Est: le Bas-Rhin. In: *Aspects de la crise et de la depression de L'economie francaise au milieu du XIXE siecle (1846-1851* (ed. Labrousse, E.), La Roche-sur-Yon, pp. 226-249.
63. A.J. Durie, and P.M. Solar, (1988). The Scottish and Irish Linen Industries Compared, 1780-1860. In: *Economy and Society in Scotland and Ireland 1500-1939* (eds. Mitchison, R.M. and Roebuck, P.), Edinburgh, pp. 211-221.
64. M. Bergman, (1967). The Potato Blight in the Netherlands and its Social Consequences (1845-1847). *International Review of Social History* 17: 390-431.
65. M. Bergman, (1967). *op. cit.*
66. J.L. Van Zanden, (1990). Den zedelijken en materielen toestand der arbeidende bevolking ten platten lande. *Een reeks repporten uit 1851,* Groningen.
67. M. Flinn, (1977). Malthus, Emigration and Potatoes in the Scottish North-West. In: *Comparative Aspects of Scottish and Irish Economic and Social History, 1600-1900* (eds. Cullen, L.M. and Smout, T.C.), Edinburgh, pp. 47-64.
68. T.C. Smout, (1977). Famine and Famine Relief in Scotland. In: *Comparative Aspects of Scottish and Irish Economic and Social History, 1600-1900 (eds.* Cullen, L.M. and Smout, T.C.), Edinburgh, pp. 21-31.
69. G. Jacquemyns, (1929). *op.cit.*
70. E. Gubin, and P. Scholliers, (1992). *op. cit.*
71. C.S. Catt, (1986). Farmers and Factory Workers: Rural Society in Imperial Germany: The Example of Maudach. In: *The German Peasantry* (eds. Evans R.J. and Lee, W.R.), London, pp. 129-157.
72. Joel Mokyr, (1980). Industrialisation and Poverty in Ireland and the Netherlands. *Journal of Interdisciplinary History* 10 (3): 429-458.

THE GREAT FAMINE
AND OTHER FAMINES
Cormac Ó Gráda

An unbroken link?

Much has been made over the last few years of the link between Irish folk memory of the Great Famine and Irish generosity towards the Third World. Sometimes the link has a prescriptive aspect, as when President Robinson tells us that "we can honour the profound dignity of human survival best ... by taking our folk memory of this catastrophe [the Great Famine] into the present world with us, and allowing it to strengthen and deepen our identity with those who are still suffering". That aspect is one stressed by the various charity agencies. But the link is also given a historical gloss. Again, President Robinson: "the past gave Ireland a moral viewpoint and an historically informed compassion on some of the events happening now".

In truth, the ties are less strong than some of us might like to think. Since I am not going to prove this rigorously, I hope I can get away with a few cameos. I was struck by the reaction of Raymond McClean, a volunteer doctor from Derry and for a time mayor of that city, when first accosted by the horrors of famine in Harbu in the province of Wollo, Ethiopia, in 1984.

"Suddenly", he remarked, "the thought struck me, right between the eyes - my God, I am walking through the Irish famine". In Dr. McClean's case the Irish Famine, then, far from being the motivating force for his time in Africa, was an afterthought. Again, I think the remarks of Bob Geldof are relevant here. In *Is That It?* Geldof says that his "point of light was an image from Michael Buerk's news report [on the BBC]. Buerk had used the word biblical. A famine of biblical proportions. To expiate yourself truly of any complicity in this evil meant you had to give something of yourself. I was stood against the wall". Nothing about the Irish Famine in Geldof's reaction to it either.

Again, thinking of the impact of the Famine on recent Irish literature in English, it is the sequence of poems by Séamus Heaney in *Death of a Naturalist* and Thomas Murphy's *Famine* which most readily spring to mind, but it turns out that the inspiration for both was not folk memory but Cecil Woodham-Smith's *The Great Hunger*, published in 1962. And I think most of what the many Irish people today know about the Famine stems not from what they heard by the fireside but from the likes of Woodham-Smith and Robert Kee. How could it be otherwise in a country where the bulk of the population is now urban and lives in areas least affected by the Famine?

I have argued elsewhere that a much more important influence on Third World giving is the Irish tradition of missionary activity far afield, particularly in sub-Saharan Africa. With the growing self-confidence of the Irish Catholic Church after the Famine whole generations of Irish people became missionaries, literally or vicariously. The link is direct in the case of Concern, a re-incarnation of Africa Concern, established by Holy Ghost Missionaries in west Africa in the 1970s, while Trócaire, another major charity agency, was created by the Irish Catholic hierarchy.

Yet here too, the story is not quite that simple. Until relatively recently, the emphasis in Irish missionary endeavour was more on souls than on bodies. In the widely-sold *Far East*, for example, in the mid-1940s there was very little about economic development or the relief of poverty, and money was sought to support personnel and church buildings. Nor, despite articles about Christ's poor in Nancheng City or how tribesmen in Upper Burma subsisted on a diet of rice, was there a single mention of the Great Irish Famine between 1945 and 1947. When precisely Irish missionaries began to take up Third World causes is an interesting topic: but it was probably in the 1960s with the changes augured in by Pope John XXIII.

Third World charities, then, have re-discovered the Famine. Perhaps the credit for being first should go to Gorta, which proclaimed in the first issue of its *Gorta News* in 1970 "Gorta is the Irish word for famine, which word itself will always stir emotive responses in Irish hearts". However, this was to be the only mention of the Irish famine in *Gorta News*, which ceased publication in 1973.

History never quite repeats itself, and the contexts of Ireland's famine and modern, mainly African, famines are quite different. Superficially, of course, all famines are alike. But the differences are worth reflecting on. Before turning to comparison, two important points. First, I readily admit that I know more about Ireland than about modern famine-stricken regions. Second, because comparison is often part of the rhetoric of condescension, it should be stressed that all famines, whatever their cause and their scope, are horrible and a scandal.

Excess mortality

In New York in May 1995 I heard the great Indian, Harvard-based economist Amartya Sen - on whom more later - declare that the Great Irish Famine may well have been the gravest ever in a relative sense. This is surely somewhat of an exaggeration. But it turns out that, by comparison, the numbers perishing in many highly-publicised Third World famines in the recent past are modest. There is no ready-made list, but I have gathered together some numbers from here and there.

For example, the official death toll in Bangladesh in 1974 was twenty-six thousand; the Sahel famine of 1973-74 killed perhaps one hundred thousand people; the famine in Darfur, western Sudan in the mid-1980s killed somewhat fewer than one hundred thousand. All three occurred in areas with a far bigger population than Ireland in 1845. One guess at excess mortality in the famine-affected areas of Ethiopia in 1973 puts it at 40,000; another puts excess deaths in Ethiopia as a whole in 1972-74 at about 200,000. In Malawi (then Nyasaland), official sources estimated that the famine of 1949-50 was responsible for the deaths of 100-200 people.

Moreover, few famines on record in western Europe matched the Great Famine in intensity: one such may have been that of *bliain an áir*, 1740-41, again in Ireland, but the evidence for this is sketchy. But neither the *années de misère* towards the end of Louis XIV's reign or the famines affecting England before the reign of Elizabeth the First were in the same league.

Now, two recent African famines are exceptional in this respect. The death tolls from war and famine in Biafra in 1968-70 probably reached a million people. Reliable estimates of famine deaths in Ethiopia in 1982-85 are lacking. In 1987 Gopalakrishna Kumar argued for a toll of at least one million, but the information reported by John Seaman suggests a smaller number. One has to reach further back for other disasters on the Irish scale. The Soviet famine of 1921-22, Stalin's Ukraine famine of the 1930s, the Great Bengali Famine of the 1940s killed many more people than the Great Irish

Famine, while the Chinese Great Leap Forward famine of 1959-62 is in a macabre league of its own.

The high mortality that followed from the Great Famine raises another related comparative issue. In his *Why Ireland Starved* (1983), Joel Mokyr proposed a redefinition of poverty in terms of the likelihood of "a random individual at a random point in time dropping below subsistence". A plausible implication of this definition, which stresses that poverty is not just about averages but fluctuations around averages, is the expectation that famines become gradually less lethal as the proportion of the population at risk declines. It follows that, considered historically, the last peace-time famines to affect a particular region should be whimpers rather than bangs.

The historian John Iliffe's claim that, between 1927 and the end of the colonial era, Africa (Ethiopia apart) saw very few "famines that kill" fits this scenario. Iliffe points to "effective government, good transport, wider markets and some increase in average wealth" as the main reasons for this. The trouble is that in many parts of Africa, alas, war and political instability brought a return of famine after Independence. We have good information on the years of "crisis" mortality in England between the 1540s and the 1860s, and this suggests that both the size and duration of famines also declined gradually over time.

Ireland's pre-Famine famines fit such a neo-malthusian pattern. Mortality from famine had been considerable in 1800-01 and 1817-19 (perhaps 40,000-60,000 in each case). The famines of 1822 and 1831 also produced excess mortality, but on a far smaller scale. Had the potato failed only in 1845 we would be saying the same of 1845. But that was not to be, and the Great Famine brought the age of famines in Ireland to a dramatic, apocalyptic, end. This underlines the ecological shock aspect of the Great Famine.

The Great Famine was also the true "last great subsistence crisis of the western world" - unless one includes the Great Finnish Famine of 1868. What of the eastern world? In recent decades famines seem to have been eradicated in China and India. It would be nice to think that just as the Irish Famine marked the virtual end of famine in western Europe, the modern famines listed above reflect the last whimpers of what John Iliffe has dubbed "conjunctural poverty" in Africa.

Mortality by age and gender

As noted earlier, estimating excess mortality during the Irish Famine is a tricky business. Estimating the relative impact of the crisis on men and women and on different age groups is more difficult still. Any such exercise for the country as a whole hinges on necessarily debatable assumptions about normal mortality rates, deficiencies in the 1841 census, and emigration before and during the Famine period. For what they are worth, the gender ratios implied in the 1851 census are given in Table 1. Since deaths in rural areas accounted for the bulk of the total, the outcome is consistent with a slight male edge in mortality during the Famine years. The relative advantage of women must be seen against their relative deprivation, marked in nineteenth-century Ireland in normal times.

TABLE 1: GENDER RATIO OF REPORTED DEATHS IN 1851 CENSUS

Year	Rural areas Male/Female	'Civic' areas Male/Female	Public Institutions Male/Female
1843	1.16	1.15	1.14
1844	1.15	1.14	1.10
1845	1.13	1.10	1.05
1846	1.17	1.07	1.09
1847	1.25	1.13	1.11
1848	1.20	1.11	1.14
1849	1.22	1.07	1.09

What of microdata? Catholic parish registers are of little use here, because even the best of them lack detailed burial data. Protestant registers can add some insight, however. Some were destroyed in the Four Courts fire of 1922, but those that survive contain the names and ages of most of the people buried. As part of a larger study of the Famine in Dublin, I have looked at the evidence on burials in several Dublin city registers. In the 1840s about one-quarter of the people of Dublin were Protestants, and the city still contained a large Protestant working-class population, as likely to be affected by the crisis as their Catholic neighbours. An analysis of the registers of three southside parishes suggests: (a) that Dublin indeed experienced some excess mortality during the Famine years, and (b) that male mortality exceeded female.

Table 2 summarises the data in the burial registers for two neighbouring parishes in the south of Ireland, those of Ballymodan and Kilbrogan in County Cork. These were then largely urban parishes; almost two-thirds of their people lived in the (economically depressed) town of Bandon. About one in four of the combined population of the two parishes was Protestant at the time. Bandon was very badly hit by the Famine. A Yorkshire newspaper proprietor noted soon afterwards:

> Bandon is a clean town, and has a rather prosperous appearance. But it suffered severely during the Famine, and one street was pointed out to us in which not a single inhabitant was left. Those who escaped death fled to distant lands, and when we saw it, every house was desolate; the garden fences were broken down; the doors and windows were partially in a state of visible decay; and the rank grass was growing about the thresholds. Altogether, it was one of the most saddening sights we ever looked upon.

Two broad impressions follow from Bandon's Protestant registers. First, the burials evidence confirms that the Famine did not kill Catholics only; among Bandon's Protestants mortality was almost 60 per cent above its immediate pre-Famine level during

1846-48. Second, the crisis seems to have increased male mortality more than female, but there were no striking changes in the incidence by age.

TABLE 2: BURIALS IN BALLYMODAN AND KILBROGAN BY AGE AND GENDER,1843-51 (Percentages in parentheses)

Age	Males			Females		
	1843-5	1846-8	1849-51	1843-5	1846-8	1849-51
0-9	34 (36)	51 (30)	24 (25)	27 (28)	40 (29)	21 (23)
10-19	18 (19)	29 (17)	19 (20)	13 (13)	21 (15)	15 (16)
30-49	8 (9)	19 (11)	11 (11)	17 (17)	13 (10)	12 (13)
50-69	13 (14)	29 (17)	24 (25)	20 (20)	27 (20)	19 (21)
70 +	12 (13)	43 (25)	18 (19)	21 (21)	35 (26)	25 (27)
Total	94	171	96	99	141	92

What of modern famines? Several studies find that male mortality rates rise more during famines. One reason for this may be the reduction in female fertility - a universal phenomenon - and an associated fall in maternal mortality. Another reason mentioned is that healthy females store more body fat than males, and therefore can withstand deprivation longer. A Trinity colleague suggests that it may have had something to do with female control of the purse-strings, but I have my doubts about that one.

The evidence on mortality by age is less clearcut. Some studies report a relative pro-child bias in intra-familial allocations during crises. In south Asia in the nineteenth and early twentieth centuries, contrary to what might be expected, the biggest increases in mortality occurred in age-groups where normal mortality was light, i.e. among older children and adults. In a recent study of excess mortality in Darfur, western Sudan in the mid-1980s, Alex de Waal found that child deaths rose more than infant or adult deaths. Overall, there are no universal patterns in the age-distribution of famine deaths.

Medicine and nosology

Relatively few died of literal starvation during the Great Famine; dysentery, typhus, typhoid fever, and other hunger-induced infectious diseases did most of the damage. Many of those contracting fever recovered from it, but it is important to remember that when the disease struck there was little that medical knowledge *per se* could contribute. Isolation in fever hospitals was the main institutional remedy for fever. In an era when cupping and leeching, mercury, opium, and a variety of powders or concoctions were the order of the day, medical 'remedies' are likely to have done more harm than good. Of course, the fact that the relevant aspects of scientific medicine were still far in the future did not prevent doctors from having a very high opinion of themselves in the 1840s. The importance of cleanliness in the homes and yards of the poor was understood, and the link between contaminated food, water and dysentery stressed but it was not so easy to do much about it.

Doctors hadn't a clue. Many believed that "the epidemic, like the ague, owes its origin to terrestrial miasms". And there were controversies between medics. In an attack on other Dublin medical men who held that famine conditions caused fever, the editor of the *Dublin Medical Press* thought "it could easily be shown that famine and destitution are more frequently the effect than the cause of fever". Medical historians have lauded the commitment and heroism of medical personnel, but results are another matter.

How much difference would better medical knowledge have made? Would the famished simply not have died of something else? These are difficult questions, awaiting considered answers. But the evidence of Third World famines may tell us something. Since the 1840s medical technology has made massive strides both in diagnosis and treatment.

First, antibiotics and anti-bacterials that can relieve typhus, typhoid fever, dysentery, and also anti-malarials have been available since the 1940s. Second, disinfectants and insecticides which help control or eradicate flies, fleas, lice and ticks that cause these fevers, have been in widespread use since the 1940s. Third, mass vaccination campaigns reduce the incidence of meningitis and measles, which are more likely to be lethal in famine conditions. Finally, though therapeutic drugs are of little help against dysentery, a major killer, ways of providing clean water are well understood. Morbidity and mortality surveys have highlighted the vital role of rehydration together with good nutrition in the recovery from dysentery. However, it has to be said that in recent famines increased resistance to commonly used drugs against bacillary dysentery has been reported. And although vitamin supplements are more easily distributed than food, the right kind of food is the main defence against xerophthalmia, scurvy, and pellagra, common occurrences in Ireland in the 1840s.

The evidence of modern famines suggests that medical technology alone is not enough to eliminate mass mortality. Almost invariably, there are time lags between detection and action, and red tape brings its own delays and conflicts. Famine-induced anaemia makes it difficult for people to absorb oral medicines. Ignorance on the part of those at risk is also a problem. Thus one suspects that in Ireland in the 1840s, as in modern Africa, modern medicine alone would have been a poor substitute for plenty of healthy food, clean clothes, proper housing, and sanitation. But given food, medicine can achieve much.

Another aspect of the medical issue is that medicine has probably shifted the class-structure of famine mortality somewhat since the nineteenth century. In Ireland, the poor were the main targets of disease such as mild typhoid fever in normal times, but during the Great Famine "when fever attacked the higher classes it was universally of a much more fatal character than amongst the poor". Its better-off victims included the Rosminian preacher Luigi Gentili, who died in Dublin in 1848 of a fever caught while hearing confessions.

At greatest risk were those who came into contact with the diseased in the course of their work. Among doctors an eminent example is the anatomist Valentine Flood, who had been working for the Board of Health in Tipperary, and who was "among the many voluntary victims offered by the profession to the Moloch of typhus contagion". With the clergy it was a similar story. It is occasionally claimed that "no priest died during the Famine", but that is ignorant cant. In fact, many priests died of fever during the Famine, as did many clergymen of other denominations.

By implication, then, another important difference between the Irish famine and today's famines is that modern elites are largely immune from the externalities once caused by famine. Modern Irish aid workers are similar enough to the priests and the medical personnel of the Famine era to carry the point. Of the hundreds of volunteers who have worked in Africa since the 1980s, one was murdered in Somalia and several were attacked by famine fevers, but it seems that none so far has died of famine-related illnesses.

The difference may have a broader implication. The American evangelist Asenath Nicholson, one of the most perceptive and humane outside observers of the Irish Famine, wrote of the "comfortable classes" of Dublin, that "whatever the hospitality they might manifest towards guests and visitors, [they] had never troubled themselves by looking into the real wants of the suffering poor". Nonetheless, the danger of contracting famine fever through contact with the poor or through inhaling infected air was a major preoccupation of those 'comfortable classes' during the Great Famine. Long before the Famine, those seeking to help the poor had found that appealing to the self-interest of the better-off in towns and cities was a good way of producing results. During the Famine it prompted the creation of fever hospitals, the financing of the Board of Health, and the control of begging in Dublin and in Belfast. One suspects that such enlightened self-interest on the part of elites counts for less in parts of the Third World today.

War and peace

The poem that begins with the line *"Ní cogadh ná caragail fhada idir ard righthibh* (it is not war nor enduring strife between high kings)" by the Jacobite Séamus MacCoitir is about another great Irish famine, that of 1740-41. Earlier famines had been the product of invasion and civil strife, but Ireland was tranquil in 1740. MacCoitir's first lines have a modern ring. "In much of Africa", writes Alex de Waal, "war has become synonymous with famine". War increases the vulnerability to famine in obvious ways such as by destroying crops, deflecting economic activity, frustrating relief, and dampening democracy and protest.

However, as in the 1740s, Ireland faced no civil war or major unrest in the 1840s. Indeed some contemporary observers spoke of a delusive calm in Ireland on the eve of the Famine. Faction fighting and rural strife, so common in the 1820s and 1830s, had been quelled by an alliance of police and priests. Ordinary crime was also in decline. The inoffensive 'rising' of 1848 lasted only a matter of hours and in any case took place when the worst of the Famine was over. Therefore disrupted communications and military distractions were not a factor in Ireland during the Famine.

This was all quite unlike the situation in so many African countries in recent decades. The horrors of Biafra, Ethiopia, or Somalia immediately spring to mind. Discussing Mozambique in the 1980s, Alex de Waal writes that some "analysis" of famine there amounts to "little more than a catalogue of Renamo vandalism". The risk of famine in Angola today is increased by the land mines (an estimated 10-15 million) left behind by the warring parties. In war-torn parts of the Sudan mines are more likely to kill cattle than people, but with potentially grave consequences too for pastoral farmers. Civil conflict also produces its IDPs (internally displaced people) and refugees. Modern famines have less to do with Malthus than with Mars.

Rich neighbours, poor neighbours

Another difference is that today's famine-stricken areas are located in the most economically backward regions of the world, where neighbouring regions seem to be nearly as poor as the region directly affected. We need only consider famine-afflicted Ethiopia or southern Sudan. But one of the striking things about the Irish Famine of the 1840s is its geographical setting: it occurred in the back-yard of a relatively prosperous region. However, economic history suggests the need for perspective here. We should not overlook the harsh conditions faced by the British poor at the time, and the poverty of even smug, mid-Victorian Britain by our own late-twentieth century standards.

The Irish Famine occurred in the back-yard of a relatively prosperous region.

How poor was Ireland in the early 1840s compared with, say, Ethiopia or Somalia today? Only the crudest answer is possible. I reckon that Irish living standards on the eve of the Famine lay somewhere between those of Ethiopia and of Somalia a few years ago, though closer to Somalia's. The comparison also suggests that the rich world today has a much greater margin to spare than Britain did in the 1840s. According to the kind of political arithmetic just described, living standards in Britain in the 1840s paralleled those of Indonesia or Egypt today. Without seeking to absolve those in power in Westminster of responsibility for not having tried harder, does this not make the persistence of famines in the Third World in the 1980s or 1990s a greater scandal than its presence in Ireland in the 1840s?

Ideology and bureaucracy

Nor is the philosophical context the same today as in the 1840s. This is an important point, but one well rehearsed elsewhere. Peter Gray has argued - and I agree with him - that "the charge of culpable neglect of the consequences of policies leading to mass starvation is indisputable. That a conscious choice to pursue moral or economic objectives at the expense of human life was made by several ministers is also demonstrable". So there is some truth in John Mitchel's claim that "Ireland died of political economy". Now, this is not to argue that a native government would have done a better job. Its heart might have been in a better place, but it would not have had the wherewithal. Daniel O'Connell's plea to fellow MPs in Westminster is apposite here: "Ireland was in their hands", he said, "if they did not save her, she could not save herself".

In India later similar attitudes would also constrain relief. There, historians insist, the machinery necessary to eradicate famine was available long before it was put into use. Why? Because those in power believed that "India would have been pauperised, its work ethos shattered, and an importunate populace of government dependents would have been created". To relieve one famine would only "have postponed a calamitous reckoning when a swollen population multiplied beyond its subsistence".

No government or international agency would argue that offering unstinting relief to famine somewhere now would only make things worse down the road. Or that famines are a divine plan to teach people a lesson. Such heartless claptrap is not much heard today. Ideology may still exacerbate crises or the risk of crises. I have given a few examples elsewhere. But history also suggests that 'good' government can help avert famines. Prompt and enlightened action in Kenya, in Botswana, and in Bangladesh in the 1970s and 1980s provide good case-studies, but the ambitious public works programme set up in the Indian province of Maharashtra (population 50 million) in the early 1970s is the best-known case in point. Indians are proud of the success of policy there, and rightly so, because the threat to a large area in a poor country was very real. In Maharashtra the output of foodgrain and pulses was 19 per cent less than normal in 1970-71, 27 per cent less in 1971-72, and 53 per cent less in 1972-73. Nevertheless, there is no evidence for a significant rise in mortality, and the birth rate fell off only slightly in these years. Now, in Maharashtra, though poor, the institutional infrastructure was there to begin with; "fair price shops" which distributed rations of grain at slightly subsidised prices were already widely established, and the public works through which most relief was administered were set up very early on. Moreover, anybody who wanted work on the works got it.

The civil servants with responsibility for Ireland in the 1840s were certainly less corrupt and more sophisticated than most Third World bureaucracies today. So were those handling the poor law on the ground, inspectors, clerks, and guardians. The same goes for the police, unloved perhaps, but pretty straight. I cannot remember a case of one of them being arrested for fraud. Ireland then is not Somalia or Zaire now. Moreover, Ireland's vibrant and relatively free press offered an adequate 'early warning system' of looming disaster and detailed information on where needs were greatest, and communications were quite good.

But was it that simple? There is the issue of the efficient transmission of aid from the centre to those at risk, or what is called 'agency'. Agency has become one of the disputatious issues in Famine studies. The claim here is a double one. First, supporters of the agency view argue that the areas with most 'voice' or influence tended to be those less affected by famine. And so, Connacht had fewest priests to plead the poor's case, Skibbereen had no relief organisations, and the Society of Friends helped Munster more than Connacht. Second, the argument goes, corruption and favouritism at local level may have meant that the allocation of funds, not their provision, was the fundamental problem. And of course, it is easy to pinpoint cases of landlords supporting their own pet projects and their own tenants and of labourers cheating on the works.

Against the objection that the clergy were there to speak up for the most needy, the 'agency' interpretation sees the priests supporting the landlord sympathetic to the Church over the landlord who refused a site for a new church. Or it mentions that some priests seemed more preoccupied by church-building than relief. Against the objection that labouring on the public works in the winter and spring of 1847 was no picnic, it objects that there were riots when the works ceased. Again Mary Daly, a cogent and persuasive proponent of the 'agency' view, writes of "undeserving large farmers" being employed at the expense of neighbours on the works and of resentment against farmers being paid for horses supplied. Such 'agency' theorising implies that ideology was no real constraint, because throwing more money at the problem would simply have lined the pockets of the wrong people - gombeen men, farmers, landlords, and so on. I still believe that in Ireland the problem was less institutional than ideological. The way was there in the 1840s, but not the will. Today, very often, where there is a will there is no way.

To argue that spending more would have made no difference in Ireland in the 1840s is to argue that what was spent saved no lives either - or else that Whitehall had managed to 'fine-tune' relief to a degree that seems quite implausible. Given its (so far) very slender evidential base, the new emphasis on agency smacks just a little of apologetics. Yet this is a controversy about which we will hear much more and which only detailed research will resolve. This is a reminder of how much work needs to be done.

Food shortages and entitlements

It is often said of modern famines that they are less the product of food shortages or poor harvests *per se* than a lack of purchasing power. In particular, economist Amartya Sen has pointed to famines in his native Bengal and in Ethiopia as products of a drop in what he calls the "entitlements" of the landless. In Ethiopia in 1973, he says, "famine took place with no abnormal reduction in food output, and consumption of food per head at the height of the famine was fairly normal for Ethiopia as a whole". Not everybody agrees, of course, but Sen's approach has the cardinal advantage of stressing the role of maldistribution or inequality, which is a key feature of every famine.

How does the cap fit Ireland? One of the most evocative images of the Irish Famine is of a people being left to starve while their corn was being shipped off under police and military protection to pay rents. Economists Jean Drèze and Amartya Sen write of "English consumers attract[ing] food away, through the market mechanism,

from famine-stricken Ireland to rich England, with ship after ship sailing down the river Shannon with various types of food". Not all the food left. Even in Skibbereen in December 1846 "notwithstanding all this distress, there was a market plentifully supplied with meat, bread, fish, in short everything". What Woodham-Smith called this "extraordinary contradiction" - images of poverty in the midst of plenty - has inspired modern artists from playwright Thomas Murphy to Sinéad O'Connor.

However, this enduring, populist image of the Famine as starvation when there was enough food to feed everybody oversimplifies. It is somewhat ahistorical in that it ignores the inequalities at the root of Irish society in normal times: before the Famine, few of those who died around Skibbereen would have been able to afford the meat, bread and fish referred to above. And dwelling on the exported grain masks the reality that at the height of the Famine grain exports were dwarfed by imports of cheaper grain, mainly maize.

TABLE 3: THE IRISH GRAIN TRADE, 1843-1848
(IN 1,000 TONS)

Year	Exports	Imports	(Maize)
1843	480	15	(1)
1844	424	30	(1)
1845	513	28	(7)
1846	284	197	(122)
1847	146	889	(632)
1848	314	439	(306)

In the history of the Great Irish Famine the issue of grain exports has more symbolic than real importance. In order to see this, let us suppose that the transfer of all the exported grain from farmers to the starving masses had been costless both in terms of resources spent on collection and future output foregone. Alas, the ensuing increased supply of food would have made only a small dent in the gap left by the blight. On the eve of the Famine the potato harvest yielded about

12-15 million tons annually, half of which went to human consumption. Thus the 430,000 tons of grain exported in 1846 and 1847 must be set against a shortfall of about 20 million tons of potatoes in those same years. Allowing the exported grain four times the calorific value of potatoes, and ignoring animal feed requirements, the exported grain would still have filled only about one-seventh of the gap left by the potatoes in Ireland in these two crucial years.

Thus, though official neglect and endemic injustice played their part in Ireland in 1846 and 1847, there is no denying that the Irish Famine was, at least in those years, also a classic case of food shortage. Only by adopting an all-UK perspective to the problem in those years might an interpretation stressing entitlements instead of food availability be defended: but that would run against two strong historiographical traditions.

A further difficulty is the long drawn-out character of the Irish Famine. The transfer implicit in the entitlements approach, instead of being a once-off surprise, would have become a kind of repeated game. The consequences for the farmers' output reaction could not have been good.

In support of the entitlements approach, deaths from starvation continued during 1848-49. Those deaths, confined largely to the west of Ireland and occurring well after Whitehall had washed its hands of the Famine, might well fit an entitlements approach better. The issue requires further analysis.

Mass emigration

All famines induce people to move in search of food and in order to escape disease; there is much movement from rural areas into the towns. But a distinction must be made between such local movements, mainly by adult males from more to less afflicted areas, and permanent long-distance migration. Mass long-distance emigration is another legacy of the Irish Famine that distinguishes it from modern famines. For many of the Irish poor in the 1840s, unlike the Somali or Sudanese poor today, mass emigration provided a welcome safety-valve.

Though data on the socio-economic backgrounds of those who died and those who emigrated are lacking, it seems fair to assume that the latter were mostly people of some modest means. For most of the landless poor, with no savings or compensation for eviction to fall back on, the cost of a passage would have been too high. The story of Anne Nowlan, a Roscommon woman who had sought refuge for herself and six children in a night asylum in Dublin's Bow Street, is interesting in this respect. Nowlan had been put into custody by the keeper for failing to account for a large sum of money in her possession. The magistrate evinced surprise at the family's condition, "while she had so much money about her". The following is Anne Nowlan's account (*Freeman's Journal, 8 May 1847*):

> She lived in the county Roscommon, and her husband held about ten acres of land, but he died last Shrovetide; she had no means of sowing a crop, and she gave up the place to a collector of poor rate, who gave her £15 for it; she got £5 for a mare, and £4 for a cow, 10s. for a cart and harrow, and more money for other things, and this made up all she had; she was about going to America, but she would not be taken with her children for less than £27.

Mass long-distance emigration is a legacy of the Irish Famine that distinguishes
it from modern famines

When her eldest boy, a thirteen-year old, corroborated her story, the
magistrate deemed it "evidently true", and discharged her.

Much has been written about the terrible conditions endured by
these 'economic refugees' and the high mortality on 'coffin ships'. But
it was not quite so simple. The American economic historian
Raymond Cohn has inferred migrant mortality on the passage between
Europe and New York between 1836 and 1853 from a sample of
contemporary passenger lists. What is most remarkable about his
findings is that neither the Irish as a group nor the famine years stand
out; the record of German ships in 1847 and 1848 was much worse,
and curiously 1849, not 1847, produced the highest mortality overall.
In Table 4 Irish ports and Liverpool represent Irish emigrants. True, the
death rate out of Liverpool was higher in 1847-48 than in 1845-46, but
the mean mortality rate was still less than 2 per cent.

TABLE 4: MORTALITY ON NEW YORK-BOUND SHIPS
1845-1853

(a)Irish Ports (b) L'rpool (c) France (d) Germany (e) London

Year	MR	Obs.	MR	Obs.	MR	Obs	MR	Obs.	MR	Obs.
1845	-	-	0.76	13	0.61	8	0.96	5	3.57	1
1846	-	-	0.91	18	1.18	11	1.07	13	1.28	5
1847	1.33	5	1.73	17	0.83	6	3.77	5	1.09	3
1848	2.74	5	1.36	34	1.35	11	3.36	2	1.04	2
1849	3.36	14	3.33	47	1.74	7	1.51	8	0.56	1
1850	1.16	7	1.54	50	0.55	3	4.41	3	1.89	2
1851	0.67	16	1.28	78	0.79	12	1.05	8	0.52	8
1852	3.59	2	0.88	67	0.74	16	0.55	5	0.96	12
1853	0.62	5	1.73	54	1.30	18	1.01	27	1.23	10

Other data, it is true, highlight 1847, and mortality among passengers who chose ships bound for Maritime and Canadian destinations (nearly half of the Irish who crossed the Atlantic in Black '47, but only 10-15 per cent thereafter) was higher than those bound for New York. Cohn's numbers exclude ships that sank or turned back and unrecorded deaths on board. Still, his results suggest that Mokyr's assessment that the overall death rate on the north Atlantic passage - "five per cent of the total overseas migration at the most" - errs on the high side.

In the circumstances, the outcome is an impressive achievement. Crucially, most of Ireland's 'boat people' eventually reached their destinations in America or Britain. None of this is to deny that conditions on the passage were harsh, or that there was exploitation of emigrants. But the fundamental comparative point to make here is that surely many of today's famine-stricken poor would give up everything in return for manual jobs and poor housing in North America, Japan, or western Europe. Reflecting on the alternative offered by Third World experience tells us that the Irish were 'lucky' to emigrate and to be allowed in, and that many more would have died in Ireland had this safety-valve not existed.

Traders and famines

As Jean Drèze and Amartya Sen remind us in their recent book, this is a topic "that is not always approached dispassionately". Part of the problem is that the empirical evidence for and against the traders is mixed. Traders make their money by moving goods from low to high price areas and by speculating correctly on price movements over time. Markets have a poor reputation in the context of Third World hunger, and I thought therefore that some musings about them in the context of the Famine would be of interest.

If markets help to even out scarcities, regional or temporal, that would seem a 'good thing'. Modern evidence also points to the disastrous consequences of governments paralysing private trade. Dréze and Sen compare policies pursued in Botswana and neighbouring Kenya during the droughts of the 1980s. In Botswana, where trade was free, a competitive food market kept price differentials across regions to a minimum. In Kenya grain movements were strictly controlled; as a result huge price differentials between regions emerged, reaching a ratio of ten to one between highest and lowest for a short time. This suggests the need for the free movement of goods. However, when there are few traders government intervention may be needed.

In Ireland in the 1840s, as in India later, officialdom had learned its Adam Smith and Edmund Burke well; allowing private traders full freedom was a major preoccupation. But what of the situation on the ground? This is a topic where accounts rarely go beyond anecdote or assertion. It is easy to find contemporary criticisms of rapacious traders. The huge rise in grain prices in late 1846 prompted one of Trevelyan's informants to tell him in late December 1846 that "£40,000 to £80,000 were spoken of as being made by merchants" in Cork, and to hope that government would intervene to check "the extortionate prices". Bessborough, the Lord Lieutenant, informed Prime Minister Russell a few weeks later that "there is no great doubt that the merchants in the great towns have taken advantage... and in some places are keeping up the prices by the most unfair means".

Such exploitation is the stuff of fiction and oral history too. Neither William Carleton's *The Black Prophet* nor Liam O'Flaherty's *The House of Gold* is directly about the Famine, but Carleton's was prompted by the Famine and both are full of famine resonances. For Carleton (referring to the Clogher Valley in the early nineteenth century) and O'Flaherty (referring to south Connemara in the late nineteenth century) the case against the exploiting mealmonger or gombeen man was an open and shut one. Yet (and maybe for that reason) hard evidence on how they behaved in crisis times is lacking. The notion that either collusion on the part of greedy merchants or extortion by remote monopoly traders exacerbated an already serious crisis is often echoed elsewhere. For example, many accounts of the greed of Malawi's maize traders in 1949 survive.

Did the traders and the moneylenders make the killings such accounts imply? Here all I can offer are some preliminary, tentative clues. Before doing so, three simple points based on the kind of elementary price theory we teach first years in UCD are worth bearing in mind. First, supply shocks would have caused monopolies to increase their prices less than firms in a competitive industry. Second, higher prices induced by supply shocks would have reduced the profits of monopolists. Third, the drastic fall in the purchasing power of their customers would have induced mealmongers - other things remaining the same - to reduce, not increase, their prices. These theoretical points suggest that some contemporary observers may have mistaken adverse supply shocks for monopoly power. On the other hand, some of the criticism may have referred to trades (such as that in Indian corn) that were unfamiliar, and therefore more amenable for exploitation.

There are several ways to interpret the claim that markets worked poorly during the Famine. The failure could have been temporary (e.g. early on, as in late 1846, when the trade in Indian meal was new); it could have been partial (for example, restricted to remote areas); or it could have been intertemporal (perhaps agents hoarded, or held on to their stocks for too long). The business accounts of Famine traders that might shed light on these possibilities have not survived, but food price data from the period are plentiful. My tentative verdict, based on recent research into this subject, is that markets worked fairly well. The analysis is quite technical so the best I can do here is to try and give an intuition.

In a well-integrated market, persistent price differences between regions stem largely from transport costs. Therefore if markets continue to work well during a harvest failure, a reduction in the price variation across regions such as counties or provinces should follow, since the fixed transactions cost element should decline as a fraction of the whole. However, if markets become more segmented, a bigger gap between regions or counties might be expected. An analysis of potato prices in hundreds of Irish towns between 1840 and 1846 suggests that the market for potatoes worked tolerably well till then. These numbers are not ideal for our purpose; they extend only as far as the harvest of 1845, the first to be affected by blight. Data on grain prices also survive, and are probably of higher quality in that a grain crop such as wheat or oats was more homogeneous than the potatoes underlying the information above. To summarise simply, my strategy here was to look for persistent gaps between grain and oatmeal prices in the main Irish cities and between such cities and London.

On the whole the trends do not incriminate Irish grain merchants. There is one tentative exception. The outcome seems to point a finger of suspicion at Cork grain merchants, since the ratio of the mean Cork to Liverpool price in late 1846 and early 1847 was considerably (10-15 per cent) higher than in the following months. But whether the outcome reflects a conspiracy on the part of Cork's grain merchants or merely delays in maize reaching Cork remains unresolved.

What of remoter rural areas? That is a question for future research; a *priori* reasoning is not enough. In late 1846, when the Famine was really beginning to bite, one senior poor law official alerted Trevelyan about how hard it was to procure retail supplies in 'remote' districts, and about the lack of small retail outlets for corn. The result was that the poor were forced to "travel considerable distances from their homes to purchase food". Given that most poor people moved about on foot, knowledge about prices was hardly perfect.

Hoarding and speculation are also part of the story. Modern evidence suggests that speculation can be destabilising in famine situations. Sen blames the situation in Bengal in 1943 largely on "speculative withdrawal and panic purchase of rice stocks encouraged by administrative chaos". Speculative withdrawals of foodgrains were also important in Bangladesh in 1974. As a crude test in my own *Ireland Before and After the Famine* I analysed seasonal movements in potato prices before and during the Famine. The test, inspired by work on late medieval corn prices, was to compare the seasonal rise in prices from autumn trough to summer peak before and during the Famine. If prices rose more from trough to peak than before, then traders were hoarding. The outcome of this admittedly limited test did not support the hypothesis that speculation made a bad situation worse.

Before leaving traders, a few comments on the provision of credit to the poor during the Famine. I will limit the discussion here to pawnbrokers. In Ireland pawnbrokers operated under relatively liberal laws, which allowed them to charge higher effective rates than their British counterparts. The result was a thriving Irish legal pawnbroking sector. Some sense of the extent of the business before and during the Famine is captured in Table 5.

TABLE 5: PAWNBROKING DURING THE FAMINE

Year	Tickets Issued	Sums Lent (nearest £)	Average (pence)
1843	10,517,022	1,458,839	33.3
1844	11,501,108	1,603,789	34.2
1845	13,039,882	1,849,758	34.0
1846	14,161,152	1,922,343	32.6
1847	11,081,865	1,293,332	28.0

Though pawnbrokers could be found throughout most of the island, there were still few in some of the most backward areas in the early 1840s. In Erris (which I think of as Ireland's Ultima Thule) 'the trade [was] unknown'. Nonetheless, pawnbrokers had made inroads into much of the west and south before the Famine, and their humble clients were from the strata most likely to be hurt by the Famine. The typical pledge was in clothing and for the equivalent of a few days' wages. Pawnbrokers' surviving records therefore allow some insight into how moneylenders fared during the crisis.

Did pawnbroking thrive during the Famine? The answer is a pretty emphatic no. In late 1848 pawnbrokers' premises in Tralee were "filled with wearing apparel of every description, homemade clothing materials, feather-beds, bedding, and tradesmen's tools of every kind". A "most respectable" pawnbroker in Fermoy related the increase in pledges in 1846 to "the destitution which commenced in that year", and the subsequent fall-off in business to the lack of suitable articles to pledge. And there is much more of that kind.

The aggregate number of legal pawn tickets fell by over one-fifth between 1846 and 1847, and the total lent by almost one-third. Neither those numbers nor individual accounts support the notion that the Famine was a golden opportunity for pawnbrokers. Surely the most plausible interpretation of them is that as creditworthiness dropped, business fell back in tandem.

Overall our findings are not robust enough to reject outright the hypothesis that the greed of millers, mealmongers, and the like exacerbated the Famine. It would be nice to think that it did, but the historian can only seek the truth. More work is needed.

A long drawn out affair

Another important feature of the Irish Famine, which of course makes it difficult to fit into any neat commemorative schedule, is that it was a very long-drawn out affair. If the second and near-total failure of the potato crop in 1846 marks the real beginning of the Great Famine, in Whitehall Russell's Whigs were already in effect declaring it over in summer 1847. The lion's share of the responsibility for relieving those affected was then turned over to Ireland.

The crisis did not end in the summer of 1847. Famine conditions lasted for a long time after, particularly in western counties such as Clare and Mayo. In January 1849 a thoroughly disillusioned Edward Twistleton wrote to Trevelyan "others might say that we are slowly murdering the peasantry by the scantiness of relief". At the level of macroeconomic indicators such as banknote circulation or company profits, the recovery took a long time to occur. The number of inmates in Ireland's bleak workhouses, a more immediate proxy for deprivation, remained high long after 1847.

Mortality did not end in 1847 either. The Great Famine therefore had more in common with the seven lean years of the Old Testament than the better-known famines of the 1980s and 1990s. One likely result is that 'famine fatigue' was more of a problem in Ireland's case. The Society of Friends threw in the towel quite early on, believing that it was the government's responsibility to do more. It is also seen in the more modest efforts of local charities such as the Society of Sick and Indigent Roomkeepers, the Mendicity Institution, and the Dublin Parochial Association.

By contrast, the Finnish Famine of the 1860s, another major catastrophe, lasted just one awful year. The latest verdict on the better-known Soviet famine of 1932-33, based on newly-available data, suggests that it too lasted about a year. Even in the case of the Great Bengali Famine, which according to Sen yielded excess deaths for several years after 1943, a recent reassessment confines excess mortality to 1943-44. And the modern famines I have mentioned typically did not last anywhere nearly as long as the Irish Famine.

Concluding remarks

In sum, then, there are similarities between the Great Famine and modern famines, just as there are similarities between the Great Famine and famines throughout history. I have tried to show that the differences are at least as interesting as the similarities, and how we can learn from both. ▨

NOTE
I am grateful to Mary Sutton for her helpful comments. I have tried here to retain the somewhat informal character of the original lecture. A shorter version of this paper, with full bibliography, is to appear in Helen O' Neill and John Toye (eds.), *A World Without Famine?* (forthcoming).

FURTHER READING

John Iliffe, (1987). *The African Poor,* Cambridge: Cambridge U.P.

Raymond McClean, (1988). *A Cross Shared Ethiopia-Derry: Famine in Ethiopia, A Personal Experience,* Ballyshannon: Donegal Democrat.

Mary Robinson, (1994). *A Voice for Somalia*, Dublin.

Amartya K. Sen, (1981). *Poverty and Famines,* Oxford: Oxford University Press.

THE FAMINE AS HISTORY

Joseph Lee

What is intriguing about the Famine as History - looking for the moment at history in the narrowest sense of the writing of history - is that although the Irish are often accused of being obsessed by history, there was extraordinarily little scholarly writing about the Famine until roughly a generation ago.

One might venture to surmise that had any other Western European people experienced the greatest single peacetime tragedy in the history of any Western European country since the Black Death, they would have devoted enormous attention to it. What is abnormal about our own reaction in the circumstances is not that we have been obsessed with the Famine, but rather that we have paid so little scholarly attention to the subject until relatively recently.

Three major works on the Famine appeared in the nineteenth century, John Mitchel's *The Last Conquest of Ireland (Perhaps)* in 1861; Fr. John O'Rourke's *The History of the Great Irish Famine of 1847, with Notices of Earlier Famines* in 1875, and W.P. O'Brien's, *The Great Famine in Ireland and a Retrospect of the Fifty Years, 1845-95,* in 1896.

None of these three authors was an academic historian. In fact the first academic history of the Famine was the volume edited by R. Dudley Edwards and T.D. Williams of University College Dublin, published in January 1956. The story of the publication of that volume has been rivetingly recorded by Cormac Ó Gráda and tells us much about the problems plaguing historical writing in Ireland as late as the mid twentieth century.

The idea of a volume to commemorate the centenary of the Great Famine was mooted by the then Taoiseach, Eamon de Valera, apparently following a suggestion by Professor Delargy of the Folklore Commission, in late 1943 or early 1944. de Valera approached the two editors of *Irish Historical Studies*, Robin

Dudley Edwards of UCD and Theo Moody of Trinity College, who agreed to edit the proposed volume. Furthermore, they agreed to produce it within a year or two, in time for the centenary. Here they made a fundamental mistake. de Valera himself was a mathematician. He had no idea of the difficulty of producing serious historical work. And to be fair to him, it was serious work he wanted, not a propaganda tract. He himself, and his advisors, especially Maurice Moynihan, the remarkable secretary of his Department, and Richard Hayes, the National Librarian, were insistent that the work should be entrusted to a trained historian who already had a reputation in the field. They wanted professional history, not polemic.

This redounds greatly to their credit, given that they belonged to the generation of the War of Independence, and were strong nationalists. Commemoration of the Famine could easily have been turned into anti-British propaganda. It tells us a good deal about de Valera's punctilious sense of scholarship - he took his responsibilities as Chancellor of the National University with great seriousness - that he resisted whatever temptation there may have been, and he would hardly have been human if there wasn't some, to exploit the opportunity for political purposes. But for all that he had little idea of what was involved in historical research

The assumption that one could produce an authoritative volume on the Famine within a year or two simply made no sense. It wouldn't have made sense even had there been trained historians available. There were none. This partly reflected the fact that modern history had barely established a foothold in Irish universities. Nineteenth century history scarcely existed, and twentieth century history wasn't taught at all. Although both Moody and Edwards were beginning to contemplate work on the Young Ireland period, particularly in connection with the centenary of Thomas Davis, they had made their reputations on scholarly studies of Tudor andearly Stuart Ireland.

Why Edwards and Moody agreed to de Valera's deadline is unclear. They may have been seduced by the prospect of Government subvention for research, which must have seemed like manna from heaven for a resource starved profession. They may also have felt a sense of obligation to try to satisfy as far as possible the Taoiseach's request. In any case, they do not appear to have explained adequately to him the impossibility of meeting the deadline.

Or perhaps, they thought, or hoped, they could meet it, or at least not miss it by much. For they did succeed in mobilising a remarkable team at short notice, all of whom would achieve academic distinction in due course, where they hadn't achieved it already. Three of them were in fact still at research student stage, Oliver MacDonagh, who would have a glittering career in Cambridge, Cork and Canberra and Tom O'Neill, later Professor of History in Galway, who produced two of the finest chapters in this or any other volume in Irish history, both derived from their M.A. dissertations on which they were put working in preparation for the volume.

Rodney Greene, later Director of the Institute of Irish Studies in Belfast, was a research student in Trinity. R.B. McDowell, already a young academic, would become a Trinity Professor, and Roger McHugh, a young lecturer in English in UCD, would duly become Professor there. The only senior scholar recruited by the editors at this stage was Sir William McArthur, a noted British medical historian. Their contributions were submitted remarkably quickly - if not in 1945 itself then in the course of 1946 or 1947.

But there were still three glaring omissions. One was a chapter on the politics of the Famine, without which the nature of the governmental response could not be fully understood. The others were chapters on the economy and population. In the event, the young Kevin Nowlan, who would become a Professor in UCD, devoted his M.A. thesis of 1950 to the politics of the Famine period, which in due course became a splendid chapter in the volume. A chapter on economics was apparently commissioned, but did not appear.

The really crucial omission was a chapter on population. In that sense, an element of Hamlet without the prince attaches to the entire project. A chapter is missing quite simply because the editors - T.D. Williams, who became professor of Modern History at UCD in 1949, replaced Moody - could not get a population historian. There was only one recognised specialist working on the history of Irish population, Kenneth Connell, and he was not prepared to do it. That reminds us how fragile was the scholarly basis at the time.

The Irish obsession with history had not translated into creating posts for historians in universities. Connell was in fact based in England at that stage. There wasn't a solitary authority on population history in any Irish university. Efforts to persuade R.C. Geary, the renowned government statistician to contribute, also failed. All this helps explain delays in the academic attention devoted to writing Famine history. Neither the government nor the universities provided the resources to permit the research.

Some of the delay in the publication of the *Great Famine* could be traced to the erratic schedules of Edwards and Williams. Had the editors been hustlers, they might have got the volume that appeared in 1956 published by 1952 or 1953. They actually went to press in late 1954, but the publication process itself took over two years. The main cause of the overall delay, however, lay more in the general state of Irish historiography at the time, than in the idiosyncrasies of the editors.

Browne and Nolan, the publishers, expected the volume to sell no more than five hundred copies. In the event it sold about two thousand copies. But their anticipated sales suggests there was no perception of any great public interest in the Famine at that time.

de Valera's own response to the volume provides an illuminating footnote, if not on famine, at least on Dev. The editors sent him a copy on its appearance in January 1956, when he was still in opposition. He replied that:

... as I heard from my grandmother many stories of the conditions during that tragic period of the ordinary people - the agricultural labourers and small farmers - in our neighbourhood I should be glad to learn how historians looking back now regard the period as a whole.

This is interesting in that de Valera, from whom one might have anticipated a narrowly nationalist interpretation, obviously thought of the Famine in social as well as national terms. Although he himself would probably have preferred a more engaged tone, he was sufficiently impressed to respond positively to the next request from the editors for support for a successor volume dealing with the post Famine period. He gave them an early appointment.

In the meantime, he sent across to the National Library for copies of the reviews in *Irish Historical Studies*, the *English Historical Review*, and the *American Historical Review*. Once he was satisfied that the volume had been well received internationally and had enhanced the reputation of Irish scholarship, he responded positively to the request for further support. He passed the correspondence on to the Department of Education, indicating his approval, and requested the Department to take up the matter with the Department of Finance. Finance stalled, delaying a decision until shortly after de Valera's resignation as Taoiseach in June 1959, and then refusing the two thousand pounds requested (over about five years) on the grounds that the national finances could not afford it. One may think what one will of the decision, but from a scholar's point of view de Valera emerges with an enhanced reputation from the whole episode.

The Great Famine is a great book. It has strong claims to be considered the single most important volume devoted to the history of modern Ireland. But there are of course defects and inadequacies, as Ó Gráda has identified. The biggest one, arising from the absence of a chapter on population, is the failure to attempt any systematic estimate of the number of dead. That estimate is essential for full historical understanding. We simply can't tell what the Great

Famine was unless we know how many died. Our assumptions make a big difference to virtually every other aspect we consider. Estimates of the number of dead in the three nineteenth century volumes of Mitchel, O'Rourke and O'Brien range from 300,000 to 1.5 million. It obviously makes an enormous difference to one's assumptions about, for instance, the effectiveness of government relief measures, or indeed the culpability of the British government, or of landlords, or of whoever else we may wish to hold responsible, if we think we are holding them responsible for 300,000 deaths, or for 1.5 million. It is, in a sense, less remarkable that so relatively little was written about the Famine than that within what was written such little attempt was made to assess its real scale.

It wasn't until 1960 that the work of the Welsh geographer, S.H. Cousens, attempted a systematic estimate of the number of dead. He came up with a figure of about 800,000. That was well short of the impression one gleans from R.N. Salaman's *History and Social Influence of the Potato*, published in 1949, or more emphatically from Mrs. Cecil Woodham-Smith's famous work, *The Great Hunger*, published in 1962. But neither of these attempted to justify their figures systematically. And even his relatively conservative estimate began to be sweated down over the next 20 years. By the mid 1970's a figure of 500,000 was being quoted by Irish scholars, though again unsupported by systematic evidence.

It was not until 1983 that the estimates began to move back upwards, with the publication of Joel Mokyr's *Why Ireland Starved*. Mokyr came up with a figure of between 1.0 and 1.1 million, allowing in addition a figure of about 400,000 for averted births - births that could have been expected but for the Famine. Despite some criticisms in detail, the consensus now appears to be that Mokyr's estimates, powerfully reinforced by the independent work of Cormac Ó Gráda and Phelim Boyle are about right. They may, of course, come to be revised in due course. Their historiographical significance is that they will oblige any revision to be based on rigorous scholarly techniques, as distinct from the ideological fancy, in any direction, of the revisionist. This, in turn, raises basic questions about the conclusions historians have reached about the scale of the Famine.

It would probably be true to say, whatever the individual variations on the theme, that Irish academic historians strove to adopt as unemotional and restrained an attitude as possible towards the Famine. The contributors to the Edwards and Williams volume were fine scholars who did enormous service to Irish historical writing. But it may be that they tended to internalise the assumptions of English historiography of their generation. Moody and Edwards did their doctorates in London, and Williams studied in Cambridge. The external examiners in all Irish universities came from England. Irish historians of that generation were bound to be conscious of the widespread English assumption that they might be prone to wild flights of exotic Celtic fancy, that any claims that sounded remotely exaggerated were in danger of being dismissed as extravagant. There may therefore have been a tendency to counter this image by insisting on the sobriety of one's scholarship.

Emotionalism had to be eschewed. This would have been reinforced by the justifiable assumption that writing on the Famine had given rise to unsubstantiated claims of mass murder. The *Irish Historical Studies* generation, and the young scholars reared in its shadow, were particularly conscious of the need to base all claims on sources - preferably archival sources. Even though *The Great Famine* contained Roger McHugh's pioneering chapter, "The Famine in Irish Oral Tradition", most contributors relied heavily on traditional type sources. They were certainly not conceived as part of the history of *mentalité*, important though the approach could be for illuminating the Famine experience, whether of policy makers, or of survivors or of victims.

All this tended to foster the type of apparently detached approach very different from the more engaged approach of Mrs. Woodham-Smith, precisely the type of emotional engagement which earned a degree of disdain from some representatives of the *Irish Historical Studies* school.

This distancing from the portrayal of the Famine as a succession of graphic horrors derived further impetus from the renewal of violence in Northern Ireland after 1969. Scholars who feared that their research might provide ammunition for IRA interpretations of Irish history, which drew heavily on the genocidal interpretation of the Famine, were naturally enough particularly loath to risk furnishing potential support to policies they detested. That encouraged a tendency towards reducing the scale of the Famine as well as exonerating British policy makers from responsibility. This was of course a highly emotional approach, but it was natural, if unscholarly, that Irish historians should find it difficult to disengage from the contemporary implications of Famine interpretations.

That is why Mokyr's contribution was so significant. Mokyr was differently positioned from Irish historians or indeed from British ones. He was an econometric historian at an American university. He came to the topic mainly as an inviting case study in economic underdevelopment, and in the relationship between population and development. He brought an established reputation, in terms of a wide range of contributions to American, British, Dutch and Belgian economic history. That reputation did not depend on the approval of peer groups in the history departments of either Irish or British universities. His peer group was the international economic history profession. His audience was therefore in certain respects different from that of previous practitioners in the field. It was important that his techniques should stand up to scrutiny by his colleagues. Once they did, he was prepared to accept whatever result they gave, without having a desired answer. He followed the figures where they took him.

That was indeed most unusual, for most of us have managed to get the Famine we needed. John Mitchel's *Last Conquest* is a classic case in point. It was originally published as a series of newspaper articles in America, written consciously for Irish Americans. Many of those Irish Americans had a need for a particular type of Famine history. Not all Irish Americans necessarily felt this need, either because they had arrived before the Famine, or because even Famine emigrants should not be wholly stereotyped and could cope with their memories in different ways. But a sufficient number of Famine emigrants are likely to have responded in a manner which left them highly susceptible to Mitchel's genocidal interpretation that "God sent the blight but the English created the Famine".

Imagine this type of Irish American reader in 1858. They would have seen things during the Famine, at whatever stage they left after 1845, that would burn themselves into their memory to the end of their days. They had been witnesses to scenes inflicted on few in history. Famine is one of the most horrible ways in which a society can decompose. It is doubly horrible because much of the decomposition occurs privately, out of sight of public witness, in the most intimate of contexts. Because Famine becomes part of family history. Eating was normally a bonding agent within the family. Food was distributed in the family. What happens when food fails? What decisions confront family members? Who distributes the food? It was normally part of the mother's responsibility before the Famine. How does she decide who gets what during famine? How does the father intervene? How are the decisions taken? Does one give most of the food to the father because he can go to the public works to try to earn the pittance to buy whatever food can be bought for the family? Remember that the public works in 1846-47 were paid on piece rates. Imagine the macabre moral economy of skeletons working for piece rates!

Does one try to give the father whatever one can in the hope that this will help him earn a bit more, and bring back a bit more food for the rest. Do you give the food to the weakest child, or the sickliest child, in the family, or to the elderly, because they need it most? Or do you calculate - and once conscious calculation enters on a matter like this, the bonds of kinship already begin to fray - they are going to die anyway, and it would be a waste to give them more?

The situation is sometimes compared with lifeboat ethics. Who do you throw overboard first when there isn't enough food to go around? The psychic pressures are even worse than in the lifeboat situation. Because now the choice of victim has to be made within one's own family. Throwing strangers overboard is one thing. Throwing children, or parents, or grandparents overboard is another. There are very few circumstances of suffering in history which cut so close to the bone as famine. And the Irish Famine was one of the greatest in modern history, claiming more victims, and lasting longer, than most of even the horrific African famines of recent decades. The fact that it lasted several years meant that the type of decision we are sketching here will have recurred several times for many of those who eventually made it to America. We must admit that we know little about the trajectories of survival in the Famine, about the numbers of survivors, including Irish Americans, who stared death in the face, but survived. How were they scarred by their experience? Some may conceivably have borne little trace of it, but it seems reasonable to assume that most of the survivors had learned more than they would ever want to know about themselves, and about human behaviour under pressure of that type.

We know from other horrible human experiences, not least the Holocaust, about some of the ways we deal with memory. Some Famine memories will have been, at an individual level, inspiring. There was a great deal of human kindness in the Famine. There was, if we are to trust many accounts, a good deal of families dying together, and a degree of solidarity among the dying. There was not a mass reversion to animal state. But there was also of course a great deal of psychic decomposition, even right down to some cases of cannibalism, even, or especially, cannibalism in ones own family. It was the cannibalism, as far as we can tell, of the deranged, of those who were themselves victims, driven mad by hunger.

If few Famine emigrants are likely to have seen such cases, many will havebrought memories of horror with them. They will have seen corpses, if not in their own dwellings, then on the roads and in the ditches. Many are likely to have felt a degree of guilt, of the type that often afflicts survivors of tragedies, not only of the

Holocaust, but of events like earthquakes and mining catastrophes. Why did you survive when others in your family did not? A sense of guilt can simmer below the surface, to perhaps breakout in uncontrollable and, to uncomprehending outside observers, in apparently inexplicable ways.

We know little about the mechanisms of coping with memory in Irish America, but we can assume that rationalisation and repression featured among them. One must be careful to pitch this analysis in terms of hypothesis, for the research required to reconstruct the mind (or rather the minds) of Irish America in these circumstances remains to be done.

But it seems plausible, on the basis of what we know about human behaviour in comparable circumstances, to assume that Irish America was a psychologically unstable mix, that it was emotionally ripe for an interpretation of the Famine along Mitchel's lines. Mitchel's genocidal interpretation that the Famine was an English conspiracy to destroy the Irish allowed, at a stroke, a 'guilt-transfer' from themselves, to the extent that it existed, to the English government. It exonerated them from ultimate responsibility for what they themselves may have done, or felt they had left undone, when they got out, having perhaps left in some cases family members behind to die.

The interpretation may have been all the more congenial because they were conscious in America of facing intense discrimination from the same class of people - white, Anglo-Saxon, Protestant - from whom they had either experienced, or imagined they had experienced, victimisation in Ireland. It would have been contrary to what we know of human nature had there not been a substantial demand for the type of interpretation immortalised in *The Last Conquest*.

Mitchel's Famine was by no means an implausible one. If few historians today would accept it in its entirety, nevertheless, it still deserves close consideration at a more complex level. The exculpatory account by Charles Trevelyan, the civil servant chiefly responsible for Famine policy, published in January 1848 as *The Irish*

Crisis, provides unconscious support for Mitchel's proposition that the Famine dead were sacrificed on the altar of political economy.

Trevelyan of course needed his famine just as desperately as Mitchel needed his - and Trevelyan readers needed their famine just as Mitchel's readers needed theirs. There is no space to ponder the psychology of English responses to the Famine, but they too are ripe for reconsideration at a deeper level than many Irish academic historians, trapped in the sometimes provincialising perspective of Anglo-Irish relations, have been ready to afford them.

Mitchel did not invent the genocidal interpretation in 1858. He had himself written along those lines during the Famine. So had many others. For the genocidal interpretation emerged very early in the course of the Famine. It is not a figment of retrospective imagination. The most celebrated Famine poem is probably that of Speranza (later Lady Wilde) *The Famine Year*. Great poetry it is not, but it captures many of the sentiments central to the genocidal interpretation:

Weary men, what reap ye? - Golden corn for the stranger.
What sow ye? - Human corpses that wait for the avenger.
Fainting forms, hunger stricken, what see you in the offing?
Stately ships to bear our food away, amid the stranger's scoffing.

These opening lines already convey the image of the dying supplying food for the English who mock their efforts even as they filch food. The primacy of English power, physical power and psychological power, is the central theme from the outset. The theme is sustained throughout, the climax in the final stanza, threatening divine vengeance for the pride - the sin of Satan - with which the rulers treated the ruled:

We are wretches, famished, scorned, human tools to build your pride,
But God will yet take vengeance for the souls for whom Christ died.
Now is your hour of pleasure - bask ye in the world's caress;
But our whitening bones against ye will rise as witnesses,
From the cabins and the ditches, in their charred, uncoffin'd masses,

For the Angel of the Trumpet will know them as he passes.
A ghastly, spectral army, before the Great God we'll stand,
And arraign ye as our murderers, the spoilers of our land.

"Murderers" does not mince matters. That was published in *The Nation* in January 1847 in what was still an early, if rapidly worsening stage, of the Famine. The theme surfaces regularly in commentary and literature during the Famine itself. The genocidal interpretation blends frequently, if unevenly, with social interpretation. It wasn't, of course, all the Irish who were dying. It was overwhelmingly the poor; Speranza herself recognises this:

There's a proud array of soldiers - what do they round your door?
They guard our masters' granaries from the thin hands of the poor.

But the social interpretation was woven into the genocidal interpretation, with the implication being that the poor would not be dying but for the fact that, as Speranza phrased it later in the poem "the stranger reaps our harvest - the alien owns our soil".

One of the most interesting challenges for Famine historiography, is to compare the prevalent interpretation among the survivors who remained in Ireland with Irish American interpretations. There was, of course, a great deal in common. It can be argued that post Famine Ireland needed a nationalist interpretation rather than a social one. For it was, after all, overwhelmingly the poor who had died. De Valera was historically correct in his reply to Desmond Williams when he referred to "the agricultural labourers and small farmers" as the main victims. Ireland before the Famine was predominantly a country of "agricultural labourers and small farmers". But this social balance was dramatically changed by the Famine. Their numbers declined disproportionately, and the agricultural labouring class, although still big, would gradually shrivel, both numerically and psychologically, despite occasional fleeting eruptions in post - Famine circumstances.

The survivors, almost by definition, were not the very poorest. Some did well out of the Famine by acquiring vacated land and adding field to field. These were predominantly the existing strong farmers. They themselves had suffered to some extent during the Famine. They too had seen horrible scenes. But they did not face starvation. They benefitted from the fact that much of the agrarian agitation directed by labourers and cottiers against themselves withered away as the Famine progressed. They benefitted too in being able to claw back conacre from cottiers when the potato crop failed. They didn't of course plan it in this way, but many of them emerged distinctly stronger, in terms of social power, after the Famine.

The highly complex social structure, with its corresponding conflict situations, was greatly simplified. Putting it rather crudely, whereas the stronger farmer may have regarded the landlord as his enemy, he was in turn often regarded as an enemy by the cottier and the labourer. There was still tension between small farmers and emerging ranchers, particularly in the West. Nevertheless, after the Famine the strong farmer didn't have to defend himself on this flank to anything like the earlier extent. In a sense the decks were cleared for action if he should choose to confront the landlord.

When that confrontation erupted during the Land War of 1879-82, it was in turn initially prompted by the fear of famine especially among the smaller farmers of the West. The failure of the potato crop in the late 1870s conjured up memories of 30 years before. The Land League , which sought to unite all farming interests, recruited the Famine as part of their arsenal against landlordism, and against the government. In these circumstances a genocidal interpretation was obviously far more useful than a historically adequate social interpretation of "Black 47".

Parnell took this as a central warning in his famous speech at Westport in 1879 when he went down to Mayo - "Mayo, God help us", which had suffered so hideously in the Famine, to pick up a crown from a potato patch. The Land League, whose president Parnell would become was concerned to foster internal solidarity among the tenants. It did not want to know about social conflict within the tenantry, or between tenants and labourers. It was dedicated to the fight against landlordism, the one conflict on which it wished to focus. It therefore needed a Famine interpretation which pitted helpless tenant against vicious landlord - an earlier round of the same conflict in which it felt itself to be engaged.

That made it necessary to imagine the landlord as the only villain, apart from the government, of the Famine piece. Conflict between farmer and landlord, and landlord as the garrison of a pitiless government, was central to the Famine it needed. This was to grossly oversimplify the real relations between government and landlords after 1845, for British officials often despised Irish landlords, whom they held responsible for allowing the country to fall into the condition which made famine possible. It also tended to tar all landlords with the same brush.

But the interpretation was not so much wrong, as incomplete. There were hideous cases of eviction during the Famine. Individual landlords could behave generously, and show solicitude for farmers, and even for the poor, but many behaved heartlessly, and some quite viciously. Nevertheless the extreme Land League interpretation of the Famine imposes an exaggerated sense of continuity, and of simplicity, on the complexities of the land question in pre-Famine Ireland, and during the Famine itself.

The nationalist interpretation of the late nineteenth century by and large reinforced the Land League interpretation. Irish nationalism, like any weaker nationalism struggling against the imperial powers overwhelming command of violence, needed internal solidarity. The weaker have no chance of winning against the stronger unless they are united. And one does not unite a movement by dwelling on earlier episodes of internal division. The nationalist interpretation, therefore required a simple British versus Irish model of the tragedy. The main socialist thinker of the time, James Connolly, naturally enough placed more emphasis on the Famine as the consequence of capitalism than of nationalism in the narrow sense. He certainly had a point, at least up to a point, but found only a muted response in the Ireland of his day. The market simply was not there for his interpretation.

de Valera's decision to commission a scholarly history of the Famine is therefore a rather remarkable one in all the circumstances. No doubt he too had a preferred Famine, but he was big enough to take the chance that historical scholarship might not deliver the desired answer. We too have our needs. The question arises as to whether the whole "revisionist" interpretation of Irish history in general, and not least of the Famine in particular, may not itself be based at least as much on the political, ideological and psychological needs of the revisionists as previous interpretations were based on the needs of their exponents. This does not mean that "revisionism" cannot contribute valuable insights, as indeed earlier interpretations contributed valuable insights.

But the first step towards a genuinely scholarly "total" history of the Famine is for us to identify what our own needs are, precisely in order to be able to guard, as far as is humanly possible, against the temptation to succumb to them. Revisionists have rightly demolished some myths of earlier interpretations. Unfortunately, however "scientific" they fancy themselves to be, they too may often be myth makers, if with a good deal less excuse than earlier writers who lacked their privileged access to an academic environment.

Is it in fact possible, for either critics or apologists, to write scholarly history about so emotive a subject as famine? I think it is, and I would go back to Edwards and Williams to support the case. That volume is the weaker for lacking something on the imaginative side. But it did struggle mightily, and often successfully, to control emotional impulses without seeking to disguise the horror of what happened. The contributors reacted to some extent against the dominant popular interpretation, but they did not fall completely into the trap of going all the way in the opposite direction.

The most difficult chapter to write from this perspective was the one on the administration of relief during the Famine. That obliged the author to confront the catastrophe in its full horror, to wade through heartbreaking accounts of human suffering. It was written by a young research student, Tom O'Neill, who was in his early twenties at the time. Had O'Neill been an instinctive "revisionist" the subject might have presented less of a challenge. But O'Neill was a strong Irish nationalist. He would later become de Valera's authorised biographer. It would have been easy for him to have played the role of the prosecuting counsel. The temptation must have been huge, and there would have been no shortage of evidence to present a plausible case.

And yet, he was a good enough historian, with both the intelligence and the integrity to say that on his reading the record that there was no policy of genocide. There was a great deal of intellectual inadequacy, and perhaps of wilful misunderstanding. There was certainly a psychology of the official mind which also found the Famine it wanted. Nevertheless, O'Neill transcended these temptations and presented the evidence in a way which still survives. Indeed, it would probably support a more censorious interpretation of government policy, even by the criteria of clinical detachment. Nevertheless, O'Neill's chapter stands as a monument to what it is possible for historical scholarship to achieve when the historians are sufficiently committed to scholarly standards to resist the temptation to find the Famine they want.

Tom O'Neill achieved that all of 50 years ago. Later generations have not always sustained similar standards. I dislike using the word maturity, because it is so habitually misused by propagandists in contemporary public discourse. Nevertheless, one may wonder if we have now reached the maturity, both as a historical profession and as a people, to fully and finally understand the tragedy of the Great Famine. If we can achieve that during these commemoration years, it may not be too much to hope that the striking surge of recent interest in the Famine will have left an enduring mark on the relationship between ourselves and our history. ▨

SELECT BIBLIOGRAPHY

Bourke, Austin (1993). *The Visitation of God? the Potato and the Irish Famine,* Dublin: Lilliput Press.

Bourke, Austin and H. Lamb (1993). *The Spread of Potato Blight in Europe in 1845-6 and the Accompanying Weather Patterns,* Dublin: Meteorological Service.

Cowman, Des and Donald Brady (eds.) (1995). *Teacht na bPrátaí Dubha: The Famine in Waterford 1845-1850,* Dublin: Geography Publications,

Eiríksson, Andrés and Cormac Ó Gráda (1995). *Estate Records of the Irish Famine: A Second Guide to Famine Archives,* Dublin: Irish Famine Network.

Grant, James (1990). "The Great Famine and the poor law in the province of Ulster: the rate-in-aid issue of 1849", *Irish Historical Studies,* vol. 27, 30-47.

Gray, Peter (1993). "Punch and the Great Famine", *History Ireland,* 1(2), 26-33.

Gray, Peter (1994). "Potatoes and providence: British government's responses to the Great Famine", *Bullán,* 1(1), (1994), 75-90.

Gray, Peter (1995). *The Irish Famine,* London: Thames & Hudson.

Hatton, T.J. and Williamson, J.G. (1993). 'After the famine: emigration from Ireland 1850-1913', *Journal of Economic History,* vol. 54(3), 575-600.

Kerr, Donal A. (1994). *"A Nation of Beggars"? Priests, People, and Politics in Famine Ireland, 1846-1852,* Oxford: Oxford University Press.

Kinealy, Christine (1994). *This Great Calamity: the Irish Famine 1845-52*, Dublin: Gill & Macmillan.

Kinsella, Anna (1995). *County Wexford in the Famine Years*, Enniscorthy: Duffry Press.

Lindsay, Deirdre and David Fitzpatrick (1993). *Records of the Irish Famine: A Guide to Local Archives, 1840-1855*, Dublin: Irish Famine Network.

McGregor, Patrick (1989). "Demographic pressure and the Irish famine: Malthus after Mokyr", *Land Economics*, vol. 65, 228-38.

Morash, Chris (1989). *The Hungry Voice: The Poetry of the Irish Famine*, Dublin: Irish Academic Press.

Ó Gráda, Cormac (1992). "Making history in Ireland in the 1940s and 1950s: The Saga of The Great Famine", *The Irish Review*, No. 12.

Ó Gráda, Cormac (1994a). *Ireland: A New Economic History, 1780-1939*, Oxford: Oxford University Press.

Ó Gráda, Cormac (1994b). *An Drochshaol: Béaloideas agus Amhráin*, Dublin: Coiscéim.

O'Rourke, Kevin (1991). "Did the Great Famine matter?", *Journal of Economic History*, vol. 51(1), 1-22.

Póirtéir, Cathal (ed.) (1995a). *The Great Irish Famine*, Cork: Mercier.

Púirtéir, Cathal (1995b). *Gnéithe den nGorta*, Dublin: Coiscéim.

Vincent, Joan (1992). "A Political Orchestration of the Irish Famine: County Fermanagh, May 1847", in Marilyn Silverman and P.H. Gulliver (eds.), *Approaching the Past: Historical Anthropology through Irish Case Studies*, New York: Columbia University Press, 75-98.

ACKNOWLEDGEMENTS

We are grateful to the following for permission to reproduce the illustrations included:

National Libary of Ireland:　　　　　2,30,33(a) and (b),35,36,
　　　　　　　　　　　　　　　　　　42,56,69,72,128,141,145,
　　　　　　　　　　　　　　　　　　149,158;

National Gallery of Ireland:　　　　　21(b),104;

National Libary of Scotland:　　　　　4,21(a),85;

Birmingham Library Services:　　　　90;

David Dickson, Trinity College Dublin:　8,11,14;

Laurance Geary, University College Cork:　97,99,106(Lancet 1832);

National Botanic Gardens:　　　　　57;

Gorta:　　　　　　　　　　　　　147;

Teagasc:　　　　　　　　　　　　28,50;

We are also grateful to the Deputy Keeper of the National Archives for permission to reproduce the letter on page 81.